THE POLITICAL
ECONOMY OF URBAN POVERTY

THE POLITICAL ECONOMY OF URBAN POVERTY

By

Charles Sackrey

W · W · *Norton & Company · Inc* ·

New York

Copyright © 1973 by W. W. Norton & Company, Inc.

FIRST EDITION

Library of Congress Cataloging in Publication Data

Sackrey, Charles.
    The political economy of urban poverty.

    Bibliography: p.
        1.   Poor—United States.   2.   Urban economics.
I. Title.
HV4045.S23   330.9′173′2   72-7377
ISBN 0-393-05472-1
ISBN 0-393-09410-3 (pbk.)

PRINTED IN THE UNITED STATES OF AMERICA
1 2 3 4 5 6 7 8 9 0

TO

Those feminists whom I know best and love the most—
Pat, Michele, Anne, Ann, Pamela, Helen, and Caroline—
and to all the others in the feminist movement who are
trying to humanize the American social order

CONTENTS

ACKNOWLEDGMENTS

I am, of course, not alone in being to an important degree a product of all I've seen, heard, felt and read, and my debt to those who have helped me see things more clearly is huge. To those who have beclouded my mind over the years with images inconsistent with the "truth" about the world, I hereby pass on the blame for all that follows which is wrongheaded and especially banal.

On the side of clarity, several people, either through their own work or personally, have helped me immensely in writing this essay. Especially useful was the following written material: David Gordon, ed., *Problems in Political Economy: An Urban Perspective* (Lexington, Mass.: Heath, 1971). Several parts of my book have profited greatly from my having read Gordon's anthology and from my using it in an urban poverty course I teach at Smith College. If what follows is of any use, we can all be grateful to Gordon for having compiled his excellent anthology, and for his lengthy comments on the articles which comprise it. I have also benefited considerably from a small, not too well known book by Thomas Gladwin, *Poverty U.S.A.* (Boston: Little, Brown, 1967). Gladwin has written eloquently about the conditions of urban poverty, and I cannot imagine anyone not finding some usefulness in his book. I have also learned a great deal from a book written by Frances Piven and Richard Cloward, *Regulating the Poor: The Functions of Public Welfare* (New York: Random House, 1971). This book on American poverty has provided all who study the matter with an especially keen analysis of the relationship between urban poverty and agricultural modernization, and the role of the Federal government in the current "relief crisis" in American cities.

Also, all of us who consider ourselves, to one degree or another, as outsiders in the economics profession, because of either our methodological stance or our politics, owe a debt to the long list of editors who have published the *Review of Radical Political Economics*. This periodical, which will be discussed later (see Chapter One, note 32), has included in its issues several articles which have been helpful to me in getting my mind straight about urban poverty. Especially useful were the following writers: Daniel Fusfeld (December, 1968), Howard Wachtel (Summer, 1971), Ted Behr, Victor Garlin, Jeff Morris, and Richard Roehl (July, 1971), and David Gordon (Summer, 1971). Though the *Review* is still struggling mightily against orthodoxy, it has provided me over the past three years with that special encouragement one gets from knowing one is not alone in the world with his or her economic heresy. For that reader who wants to learn economics anew, it is probably a much better idea to start with the kind of material published in the *Review* than with the conventional materials usually taught in college economics courses. Quite simply, there is a spirit of adventure and basic inquisitiveness in the *Review* which has long since been lost by the mainstream of American economic inquiry.

Of course, there are numerous other books and articles which help one in writing an essay like this; most of them are cited in footnotes, and all are included in the bibliography at the end of the book.

More direct aid came from my student assistant for two years, Pat Younger, an economics major at Smith and an indefatigable researcher and typist. Pat has helped me on this project in several ways: she typed two drafts of the manuscript, the first from a draft which in places probably looked like a cuneiform document from ancient Babylonia. But my debt to her goes beyond this. Pat is typical of so many of my students at Smith, whose honesty and good-naturedness have made me more honest and easier to get along with than I would probably be in many other places. To her and to them I owe an enormous debt, for teaching them and learning from them has helped me keep my spirit alive, enough at least to write this book. We professors are, at last, dependent absolutely on our students: they listen to our endless droning, they respond to our tedious questions, they allow us to witness vicariously the great drama of being young, healthy, and (relatively) unprogrammed, and, to top it off, they pay the bills! Thank you, Pat, and all the others.

Also, I am grateful to Mark Aldrich, a fellow I teach with at Smith. He is a very close friend, and I tell him all. Consequently, I have talked with him about all this, he has read all of the manuscript, and he has helped me immeasurably in getting it all together. In addition, Mark's contempt for anything that smells of bureaucracy has, over the years, helped me maintain a concentration on the other aspects of Smith College—students, and things to read and think about—and for that I am eternally grateful. Also, he is a better historian and theorist than I am, and that has been quite helpful at times. I am also grateful to another friend of mine at Smith, Phil Green, from the government department. Phil knows more information than anyone I can think of, and he is a much keener logician than I am. Consequently, I draw from this friendly reservoir almost every time I write something. I have talked to Phil several times about modern pluralism and its relationship to liberal reform in this country; in addition, he has read parts of Chapter 4 and has helped me put much of the material on politics together in my mind and on paper. Another friend, Larry Sawers of American University, has read the entire manuscript, and his comments have been of considerable help. Larry takes a somewhat different methodological position than I do, and his reading the manuscript with a slightly jaundiced eye led to a much clearer understanding on my part of most of the issues I take up in the book.

Another close friend over the years, Ann Jones, has also read the manuscript, and her comments, especially those concerning the last chapter, have been invaluable. In fact, an earlier conversation with Ann some two years ago convinced me to try such a book as this, and her confidence that I had something worth saying on the matter of urban poverty was a key determinant in my actually undertaking the writing.

I am also grateful for many conversations and a growing friendship with the Cooneys, some rural friends of mine: Blanche, Elizabeth, Eliza, Jimmy, and Gabriel. Their collective commitment to nonviolent political change has taught me a good deal about the limitations of my own political inclinations. Besides that, they are romantics, my *most* favorite kind of people.

I also thank another woman in my life, the one to whom I am married—but how does one express gratitude to one's mate on a page like this? I shall write a poem someday, expressing thanks for, among other things, reading all this stuff twice, commenting upon its weak places, and, in general, playing a crucial role in my finally getting it down on paper. Moreover, Pat's involvement in the politics of the feminist movement, and her work in helping to organize and run a local "women's center," have demonstrated to me how important the reform elements of the women's movement have been to the direct recipients of its benefits. Trying to come to terms with the net benefits of "liberal reform" has been a problem for me over the years (as the following pages will show clearly), and being so close to the women's movement has certainly lent clarity to my thinking about the entire issue. In addition, along with the black liberation movement, the women's movement probably represents this society's last chance at being civilized, all others having been lost to some larger goal (like efficiency, war, or consumerism). Thus, the bit of optimism which I get from vicarious participation in the movement has made these pages less dark than they might otherwise have been.

Finally, I should like to thank my editors, James Mairs and Emily Garlin. They have been helpful and thoughtful during the past year, and their suggestions have in some instances been crucial in making my manuscript come out as I wanted it to.

So, what follows comes from a number of varying directions, and who knows who should be blamed for the bad parts, or who should take credit for the good ones?

THE POLITICAL
ECONOMY OF URBAN POVERTY

INTRODUCTION

The poverty of millions of urban Americans is among the most offensive characteristics of a social order which claims to itself and to a world audience to have discovered the true path to material welfare. At this very instant, old people, children, black people migrated from depressed rural areas, deserted women, and others for whom our social system has failed to provide adequate opportunity sit and watch an unprecedented flow of material wealth pass them by. Until all Americans are given the same chance that the rest of us take for granted, we can lay no claim to having solved the fundamental duty of a civilized society. And all our vast wealth, which we flaunt as evidence of our greatness, will continue to pile up in ever higher monuments to our insensitivity toward those who have been denied their share of the world's gaudiest pie.

This book is an introduction to the study of these urban poor and possible solutions to their most serious problem. It is a work in "political economy," in the sense that it combines an analysis of the economic factors which cause poverty with a discussion of the implications for political activity which are inherent in all such analyses. It should be mentioned here that others have used the term "political economy" in different ways then it is used in this essay; therefore, my use of the term should be distinguished from the definition given by other economists. To some, political economy is essentially an *interdisciplinary* undertaking, with special emphasis on the findings of all the social sciences. To still others, political economy is a term used to describe those studies of the economic order which are especially concerned with the accumulation and use of political and economic power. None of these definitions, of course, is any more valid than the others. Indeed, to Jacob Viner, a famous American economist of the nineteen-thirties and forties, economics was defined as "what economists do." I suppose the same principle applies to political economists as well.

In many ways, this book differs from the typical academic treatise on a social problem. First, in a few places, I emphasize my own confusion about issues discussed; further, I tend to elaborate the enormous methodological problems inherent in any study of human behavior, rather than mention them briefly and plow ahead. Indeed, as I read back over these pages, I find that at several places I hint that the enterprise of "social science" may be little more than the monumental pretensions of social theorists, whose dreams of an objective study of human events are sheer fantasy. Second, I have written a relatively personal final chapter about radical politics and urban poverty, in which I detail some of the more important facets of my own response to American social problems during the past decade. Finally, these pages are, in places, polemical, and, one may even argue, strident. I will not apologize for this style, for it is a major consequence of my having watched, with varying amounts of dismay and despair, this nation gradually and systematically destroy many of the latest, most ill-prepared migrants to most of its metropolitan areas. For those who want their economics served up sterile and "objective," I can only suggest they turn elsewhere. My principal commitment, as an economist and as a writer, is to an honest elaboration of what makes sense to me; in the context of this book, what I have seen has made me sad and has made me angry, and these pages *intentionally* reflect such feelings.

The basic conclusions of these chapters are easy to summarize: 1) There is a great deal more urban poverty than government statisticians (and others) have led us to believe, principally because of the primitive methods they employ to measure it; 2) the problem is disproportionately one of black people; 3) the principal proposals implemented in the past for abolishing urban poverty have failed miserably in terms of their own goals; and 4) the most difficult task facing one who would abolish poverty is to choose between the two opposing political responses —liberal reform and revolutionary change—both of which have enormous inherent limitations. I shall spend a good deal of time on these political possibilities and in so doing will try to bring some light to a very, very clouded issue.

To many of my peers, close friends and others, the nineteen-sixties were a decade of persistent frustration over the very obvious fact that liberal reform of the American social order was a dismal failure, especially when measured in terms of the lives of our black and white sisters and brothers at home, and our Vietnamese sisters and brothers so far away, who were dying, slowly or otherwise, because of the way our system functions. Because of this frustration, some of us turned toward revolution, in one way or another. Some went underground to blow up buildings, shoot policemen, or raise a sporadic, nomadic kind of general rebellion. Some, like myself, sat on the sidelines, in terms of the more revolutionary political styles, though secretly believing that the revolutionary was probably alone in doing anything of importance to aid the poor, the black, or the Vietnamese. A few self-proclaimed revolutionaries remained in the middle of the conventional political fray, seeking to speed up the process of liberal reform or undermining the system from within. Some left the country; others entered into various communal arrangements; some took to drugs, Oriental mysticism, or a combination of both; and so on. The point is that no one on the political left in this country failed, at one time or the other during the nineteen-sixties to ask himself or herself the following question: Should I work to change the system in the *middle* of it, or should I blow the system to kingdom come (figuratively or literally)? The final two chapters here ask that kind of question about urban poverty: Can it be abolished in the American capitalist system by liberal reform . . . and what happens if it can't?

A subtheme is also present here, interwoven throughout, sometimes becoming explicit (as in Chapter 3), but always present in the background. It concerns the relationship between the method of studying urban poverty and the kind of policy prescriptions which the "experts" have in hand when they finally emerge from their academic catacombs and seek to change the world. In most contemporary social science analyses, there is an alleged distinction between the "positive" aspects of the work and the "normative" ones. The former are concerned with the study of "what is," the latter with "what ought to be." Indeed, given the canons of modern science, most people who study the social order in an academic environment present themselves as "objective scientists" whose dispassionate approach is the *only* legitimate one. So-called normative questions, like "How *well* does the system deliver *necessary goods* and *services* to *all* the people," are considered questions of interest—usually but not always—but not legitimate questions for a scientist *qua* scientist. As a consequence of this particular methodological stance, most contemporary economists take, *as given*, the general characteristics of the economy—the way output and wealth are distributed, and the political system, are examples here—and try to determine *how* the systems works, rather than spending their time trying to determine why it fails so completely to deliver many crucial services that a wealthy *and* civilized society would be expected to provide. What is important about all this, in the context of this book, is that a major result of the current methodological habits of American economists is the tendency for them to take a "liberal" political stance (a liberal is defined here simply as one who believes the American social order can be made fundamentally better through reform politics).[1] Since most American economists typically know little about how other kinds of systems might or do work, concentrating as they do on how this one functions, their policy prescriptions for solving poverty, or other social problems, are usually mild suggestions for minor changes in the overall political-economic system. It is quite important that those who seek to know about urban poverty also know how the experts in the matter develop their particular wisdom. American social scientists, and especially economists and sociologists, have done the overwhelming majority of descriptive and analytical work on poverty; therefore, all of us should know something about the frequently unstated point of departure for their analyses.

However, before we take up these difficult questions of anti-

1. Such a liberal political style should be familiar to most of us, either because we have adopted liberal reform as our own politics or because we have seen other liberals in action (like Senators McGovern and Edward Kennedy, academic liberals like John Kenneth Galbraith and Arthur Schlesinger, Jr., or multimedia liberals like McGeorge Bundy). Important in this book is the distinction between liberal reform and "revolutionary politics," where the clear aim of the latter is, as Marx put it, "an expropriation of the expropriators."

poverty politics, and the methodology of studying the problem, it is necessary to provide a substantive base for the discussion: a detailed description of the problem and some explanations of what caused it. The following two chapters are intended to provide that foundation.

Chapter One

COUNTING THE URBAN POOR AND EXPLAINING THEIR POVERTY

What are the dimensions of urban poverty? How many people are poor, and how did they become so? What can be said about poverty statistics? These are some of the questions I attempt to answer in this chapter. In addition, the discussion concerns the *causes* of poverty, and I will review some of the more popular explanations given by economists. To be sure, the answers given here are limited by the data available, and, more important, they are limited by the incapacity of the human mind to encompass such broad patterns of human behavior. Somewhere, encapsuled in the corner of a library, nervously pecking away at a typewriter, is someone whose findings may make obsolete all that is said here, or will, at least, substantially modify it.

Over the years, the study of poverty has been especially subject to these kinds of reinterpretations; for example, Oscar Lewis's work on Mexican and Puerto Rican families, from which he developed his "culture of poverty" thesis,[1] and Michael Harrington's *The Other America*,[2] which popularized Lewis's framework and, legend has it, introduced liberal America to the larger dimensions of poverty, were both books which caught us all unaware. Indeed, these two writers, and their critics, importantly redefined our understanding of poor people and their problems. Such books are being written now and have not yet been published, have been written and are being ignored, will be written and/or published and ignored; thus, no matter how hard we work, no matter how careful our endeavors, how diligent our research, the great drama of human behavior is subject to as many different interpretations as there are people trying to interpret; so take this discussion, at best, as tentative.

I. The Number of Urban Poor

How many people living in American metropolitan areas are "poor," and what kind of people are they? What race, what sex, what age are they? In what occupations and industries are they employed? Here is a very brief review of some of the data, and reflections on them. Using data for 1968,[3] we find the following:

1. On the basis of the 1968 Social Security Administration definition of poverty (defined below), there were 12.9 million poor people in metropolitan areas during that year. Of the total, 67 percent, or 8.6 million, were white; the remaining 4.3 million were nonwhites (in the figures given here and below over 90

1. Lewis first introduced the "culture of poverty" idea in Chapter 1 of *Five Families* (New York: Basic Books, 1959). In later books, which reflected a similar research method, he developed in greater detail the general characteristics of his "culture of poverty" thesis. See especially the Introduction to *La Vida: A Puerto Rican Family in the Culture of Poverty* (New York: Random House, 1966), and *The Children of Sanchez* (New York: Random House, 1961), pp. xxiv–xxxi.

2. New York: Macmillan, 1962.

3. Anthony Downs, *Who Are the Urban Poor?* (New York: Committee for Economic Development, 1970). Unless otherwise indicated, the data here are from Downs's book.

percent of those listed as "nonwhites" are black people). This, of course, means that urban poverty is *absolutely* a greater problem for white people. However, *relatively* it is a greater problem for blacks since blacks comprised 16.8 percent of the total population of urban areas, but about 30 *percent* of the urban poor (in 1970). Moreover, in *central cities* of metropolitan areas, nonwhite people comprised an even greater proportion of the poor (43 percent). This figure indicates that the closer one gets to the center or "downtown" of the typical urban area, the more likely one is to find poor, black people. Much more will be said about this matter later.

2. Forty-two percent, or 5.4 million, of the urban poor are children under the age of eighteen years. About 46 percent, or 2.5 million, of these children are nonwhite.

3. Eighteen percent, 2.4 million, of the total urban poverty population are people over sixty-five years old.

4. About 2.3 million female-headed poor families, including 2.9 million children under eighteen years old, live in urban areas.

5. Of the urban poor, 3.2 million, or 24.5 percent of the total, live in families headed by a male who is actually regularly employed.

6. Typically, nearly one-sixth of the urban labor force is unemployable for over six months of each year because of health problems which keep them out of the work force.[4]

Consider a different look at these figures. Taking households, rather than individuals, we find that 18 percent are headed by people too old to work, 15 percent by people too sick to work, and about 25 percent by people who work but whose annual income is below the poverty income level. This means that roughly 60 percent of urban poor families are incapable of making an adequate income because of the relationship to the labor market of the potential breadwinner: they are headed by people who are too old or too sick, or who work at extremely low-paying jobs. The remaining two-fifths of the urban poor are comprised of households headed by 1) employable women who can-

4. Howard Wachtel, "Looking at Poverty from a Radical Perspective," *Review of Radical Political Economics*, Summer, 1971, p. 4.

not enter the labor market either because of the lack of jobs or because of inadequate child care facilities—or both; 2) employable men without jobs; and 3) others who probably won't get a job whether they are looking for one or not. The principal implication here, of course, is that urban poverty *simply cannot be interpreted as the fault of the urban poor*. Since this feature of the problem bears heavily on my later discussion, it should be kept firmly in mind. In any case, taking the rough 1968 data, and doing nothing to them, we find that urban poverty is the *special* problem of blacks, workers in low-wage industries, old people, female-headed families, and children.

What can one make of such an abstraction? "Thirteen million poor people in the cities." What does that *really* mean? First, and foremost, I would argue that it means nothing as a simple number. Indeed, since no ordinary mind can encompass that much deprivation, that much suffering, that much human waste, some people use poverty data as a convenient way to deal with the problem at a level of abstraction which is, quite simply, psychologically tolerable. Let me try to explain why I make such a harsh judgment concerning these data by describing the way in which the figures are compiled by the Federal government. The story goes something like this: [5] Each year, the U.S. Social Security Administration attempts to determine how much income it would cost an individual or families of varying sizes to purchase food adequate for an absolutely minimum diet, but one which the U.S. Agriculture Department estimates would not provide most families with a diet consistent with good nutrition. This figure is then multiplied by three, the assumption being that the food costs of a minimum diet are approximately one-third the total costs of a minimum income. The figure is adjusted for region, family size, and other similar variables, and the "poverty income" can then be calculated for the typical urban family of four. The figure was about $3,550 for 1968. The $3,550 income level—or the applicable one—is then compared with census data, and one can derive the number of "poor" simply as those

5. For more details on the matter, see Mollie Orshansky, "How Poverty is Measured," *Monthly Labor Review*, February, 1969, pp. 37–41.

households where the income is less than the poverty-income level.[6]

There are quite apparent limitations of these data that need mention, and I must point out that I am not the first to call attention to their shortcomings. However, I do not plan to follow the practice of countless other writers in this area who bemoan the enormous limitations of poverty data, then write books and articles based quite squarely on those data. In this book I will argue that the poverty counters should be virtually ignored, and here are some reasons why.

In general, the most serious problem, as I understand the figures, is that they underestimate the dimensions of urban poverty, for they do not take into account the other characteristics of being poor besides the most obvious one of not having enough income. In addition to underestimating the difference between the absolute income of poor people and others, the data also ignore the crucial fact that *relative to everyone else,* poor people are typically able to enjoy fewer goods, do fewer things, and achieve fewer goals than all those above them in higher-income classes. What follows, therefore, explains two things: 1) the many limitations of absolute income figures, and 2) the different perspective on poverty which flows from a concentration on relative income data.

PROBLEMS WITH ABSOLUTE INCOME FIGURES

We can set the stage for discussing absolute poverty data with a simple example: Assume two urban families of four, one with an income of $3,550, thus statistically a poor family, and the second with an income of $10,000. A great deal of empirical evidence would predict that the first family would tend to live in the urban core, the second in the suburbs. Or, at least, common sense would suggest that the two families live in different neighborhoods, one clearly better than the other. The difference here

6. Using the government's 1969 "poverty income" of $3,743 for an urban family of four, there were 12.3 million poor people in urban areas in 1969, "down" from 12.9 million in 1968; however, due to recent Nixon Administration policies, and for other reasons, the number of urban poor increased to 13.7 million in 1970, the first increase since 1959. More about this later.

is quite significantly related to the income deprivation of the poor, for there is a relatively meager flow of public and private services to poor neighborhoods. The evidence clearly shows—in fact, it screams out—that the poor are provided with low-quality services in the following areas, among others:

Health Care

In general, both the availability and the provision of health care are better the higher the income a family receives. David Gordon's anthology *Problems in Political Economy: An Urban Perspective* (see my Acknowledgments) includes one study showing that in Chicago there are roughly twice as many doctors per one hundred thousand people in nonpoor areas than in poor ones. Forty percent of the Chicago poor do not have a personal physician, and the rest, in general, get inadequate and incomplete medical care. Other studies cited by Gordon show that, when compared to nonpoor sections of the city, the poor areas in Chicago had a 60 percent higher infant mortality rate, a 200 percent higher incidence of premature births, twice as many cases of tuberculosis per year, and 550 percent more cases of venereal disease. In Los Angeles, residents of Watts, who comprised only 17 percent of the population of that city, had 48.5 percent of the amoebic infections, 44.8 percent of the cases of whooping cough, 46 percent of the cases of venereal disease, 65 percent of the tuberculosis cases, and a death rate 22.3 percent higher than that of Los Angeles residents outside Watts. Chicago and Los Angeles are not exceptional. Fred Anderson, writing in the *New Republic,* found that in urban slums "There is three times as much heart disease, five times as much mental disease, four times as much high blood pressure, and four times as many deaths prior to the age of 35 as for the nation as a whole."[7] Anderson also discovered that the typical infant mortality rate in a northern city was the same as that in Ecuador, one of our southern neighbors which we ordinarily think of as relatively underdeveloped.

7. Fred Anderson, "The Growing Pains of Medical Care," *New Republic,* January 17, 1970, p. 16.

And there is more, for the interested observer. Let me quote from Gordon on an especially tragic dimension of the health of poor children: "Many ghetto residents suffer from disease unique to their environments. For example, at least 400,000 poor children had lead poisoning in the United States in 1969. . . . Also, there were 14,000 cases of rat-bite in the United States in 1965, most of these in ghetto communities where rats feast on garbage and hide in rotten buildings." [8] Gordon also mentions, as endemic problems for poor people who are sick, 1) the fact that the health care they receive is slow, unfriendly, and ordinarily located long distances from their homes; and 2) the very obvious fact that there is considerably less *preventive* medicine available to poor people than to their richer neighbors. The point is that poor people, for many reasons, are more likely to get sick and less likely to be healed when they are sick.

There are, in short, two health programs in this country, one for the poor, another for everyone else, the former clearly an inferior one. Think about it: to be poor is to have little income; also, it is to have little health care. So subtract from the poor family's income, when compared to that of the less poor, some amount reflecting the poorer flow of medical services.

Education

Consider this second example of the additional disadvantages of the poor which make their real income lower than it appears. There are more studies than one could read in a lifetime indicating that the quality and quantity of education received by American youngsters depends, mostly, on the income and educational background of their parents (the latter, of course, being determined mostly by *their* parents' income).[9]

8. Especially useful in Gordon's book (Lexington, Mass.: Heath, 1971) are pp. 323–326 and excerpts from Barbara and John Ehrenreich, *The American Medical System: Power, Profits and Politics* (New York: Random House, 1970), pp. 336–347 in Gordon. See also John Kosa *et al.*, eds., *Poverty and Health: Sociological Analysis* (Cambridge: Harvard University Press, 1969).

9. As a start in this area, see W. O. Stanley *et al.*, *Social Foundations of Urban Education* (New York: Dryden Press, 1956). Also, one might benefit from reading parts of the "Coleman Report"—James S. Coleman *et al.*,

And, as a prime determinant in the perpetuation of poverty, there is also ample evidence to show that a poor person, especially if she is black, will receive fewer benefits from any given amount of education, no matter what quantity and quality.[10] If you are wealthy, chances are you will go to a suburban school, adequately financed, with the latest equipment, the best teachers, etc. Upon graduation you will go to one of the better colleges or universities, where, *presumably*, the instruction, books, and facilities are superior to those at the junior colleges, where the poor, or not so rich, go if they go at all. The point is that the greater the resources your family has as you go to school, the greater the school system will add to your capacity to make income when you graduate. (And this will be true, usually, even if you are relatively dull when compared to graduates from less prestigious schools.) To be poor is to get inadequate, or relatively inadequate, educational services, and about this matter there is very little debate.

Peter Schrag, long a student of the American urban scene, has neatly summarized the essence of the matter as regards black students as follows:

> No one needs another set of statistics to prove that American Negro children—and many others—are being miseducated. . . . In the twelfth grade more than 85 per cent of Negro children score below the average white . . . on tests of achievement, their dropout rates are higher, and their self-esteem is lower. . . . there is not the slightest doubt that, if they measure education achievement and if they predict future success in school and college (as they do), then the children of the poor minorities in America perform well below average. What the new statistics do provide is solid evidence for the repeated assertion by civil rights leaders and others that what children learn in school are the rules and attitudes of second-class citizenship, and that the

Equality of Educational Opportunity (Washington, D.C.: Government Printing Office, 1966), and his critics, for example, Samuel Bowles, "Toward an Educational Production Function," in W. Lee Hansen, ed., *Education, Income and Human Capital* (New York: National Bureau of Economic Research, 1970).

10. The next chapter contains more information on the relative income of urban black people.

school is a highly effective mechanism not only for advancement but for selecting people out.[11]

Thus, one of the grand ironies is that the American public education system—aimed originally at providing ample opportunity for all—has, at least in recent times, become another of the social institutions which guarantee that those on the bottom stay there. So, again reduce the real income of the poor, and the closer to the bottom they are, the greater your reduction should be.

Treatment Before the Law

To be poor is also to be treated unequally before the law. This particular aspect of the problem is given special emphasis here since it is frequently excluded from most analyses of poverty, even those which attempt to rise above the limitations of poverty data.

Let's look once again at our hypothetical urban family of four with the $3,550 income. The odds are that it will be provided with lower-quality legal services for the normal affairs of living: divorce, petty spats with friends or neighbors, tenant-landlord disputes, and consumer protection are examples. In the event of more serious wrongdoing, however, the penalty for being poor becomes even greater, for the courts and the rest of the legal system simply do not treat different income classes the same way. This argument has been made by numerous observers in the past, and among the most persuasive is David Gordon.[12] Gordon discusses American crime in the context of the class structure of American society; what follows has been influenced by the general framework of his argument and others similar to it.

To begin with, it is instructive to discuss briefly the way in

11. Peter Schrag, "Why Our Schools Have Failed," in Marilyn Gittell and Alan Hevesi, eds., *The Politics of Urban Education* (New York: Praeger, 1969), pp. 308–309 (published originally in *Commentary*, March, 1968, pp. 31–38).

12. David Gordon, "Class and the Economics of Crime," *Review of Radical Political Economics*, Summer, 1971, pp. 51–75. An excellent bibliography is provided at the end of this article.

which our legal system reacts to the crimes of the *non*poor. Probably we are all aware of how poor lawbreakers are treated, principally because their crimes are the source of considerable news coverage, as is their treatment in prison and the conditions of the prisons themselves. Everyone hears about the brawl in the bar, and the mugging after dark, and we are all treated daily to rhetoric about our national commitment to "restore law and order." Too few of us, however, know about the crimes of those whose lawlessness and disorder is confined to the shady, subterranean strata of the American corporate world. A few comments about the kind of crime flourishing in this quarter will help emphasize just how unequal our treatment of people before the law can be.

Consider, for example, the case of a rich corporate criminal, the famous Texas swindler Billie Sol Estes. During the same week that Estes was sentenced to fifteen years for having embezzled *at least* twenty-four million dollars from Texas ranchers, farmers, and banks, a young Mexican-American in Austin, Texas, was sentenced to fourteen years in prison for breaking into a suburban department store.[13] Estes was initially convicted in Federal District Court on March 28, 1963, on four counts of mail fraud and one count of conspiracy. However, due to expert legal advice—the kind of legal advice available to rich corporate criminals—Estes was able to avoid imprisonment until March 6, 1965, two years after his original conviction, and he entered prison only after several attempts to get the U.S. Supreme Court to reverse the decision had failed. Estes was released in early 1972, after having served about six and a half years of his fifteen-year sentence.

A more recent example of how corporate criminals are treated before the law is also instructive here. Frank Sharp, another convicted swindler from my home state of Texas, was fined five thousand dollars and given a three-year *suspended* sentence for building an insurance empire through several illegal methods,

13. The reader will have to trust my memory on this incident. I read of it in a local newspaper while living in Austin, Texas, and the story had an enormous impact on me, especially when I compared the young Mexican-American's sentence to that given Estes. The information on Estes comes from several articles in the *New York Times*, beginning in March, 1963.

involving millions of dollars, various insurance companies and banks, and several individuals in Texas. Interestingly, he was treated relatively lightly by the courts apparently because 1) he promised to be a state's witness for the Republican Justice Department against several prominent Democratic politicians and others also involved in his schemes; 2) the Federal judge at the trial apparently made a distinction between real, punishable theft (i.e., burglary) and the "complicated business transactions" which had gotten Sharp into trouble; and 3) (perhaps) the judge had been previously associated with a law firm which at one time had provided legal services to Sharp.[14]

In essence, we treat the crimes of the poor differently from those of the rich by defining those of the poor—typically theft, armed robbery, burglary, or similar felonies—as especially heinous, and dismissing many of those of the rich as "part of the capitalist game." Sociologist Edwin Sutherland, in an important but relatively neglected book, *White Collar Crime*,[15] analyzed the criminal behavior of corporation employees, concentrating on crimes in the seventy largest firms through 1956. His findings, taken here from a condensed version in the Gordon anthology, bear on my point.[16]

There are various laws regulating business firms, ranging from those against price-fixing and trade violations to crimes against labor, such as union-busting, blacklisting, and yellow-dog contracting. Sutherland found that each of the leading corporations had an average of fourteen such crimes against it, that 98 percent were repeaters, that 90 percent were habitual criminals, that forty-four of the seventy firms had committed unfair labor practices against their workers, five of which were violent crimes in which workers were killed or wounded by corporation strikebreakers. More specifically, Sutherland found that Henry Ford once hired six hundred thugs in an attempt to force Ford

14. James Reichley, "The Texas Banker Who Bought Politicians," *Fortune*, December, 1971, pp. 94–99, 143–146.

15. Edwin Sutherland, *White Collar Crime* (New York: Dryden Press, 1949).

16. Sutherland's principal conclusions are summarized and updated in Ferdinand Lundberg, *The Rich and the Super-Rich* (New York: Bantam, 1968), pp. 113–154.

workers to submit to his dictatorial views on unions; he also found that the organizer of the Goodyear Tire and Rubber Company was an embezzler. Indeed, Sutherland discovered much more, but these examples should make his point. To such a list, of course, one should add Matthew Josephson's principal "Robber Baron," John D. Rockefeller, an habitual criminal, whose whole life was, in my judgment, devoted to a primitive, aggressive submission of everyone and everything who got in the way of his attempt to monopolize every stage of the national oil industry.[17]

A final example should bring home the point. It was discovered in 1961 that the heavy electrical equipment manufacturers had, for several years, been selling equipment at rigged prices, in direct violation of the criminal provisions of the Sherman Antitrust Act.[18] One leading conspirator, William Ginn, a senior vice-president of General Electric, had been personally involved in the conspiracy and perfectly aware of how he and executives from twenty-eight other companies had agreed to fix prices on their products. One result of their conspiracy was that several private and public power companies were forced to pay rigged prices for about fifteen billion dollars' worth of turbines and related equipment over a period of at least eight years. Of course, this kind of price-fixing led to higher prices for electricity in many areas of the country.

As a consequence of these crimes, Ginn, along with six other executives, was put in jail for *thirty days*, and the companies were fined varying sums of money. Compare this thirty-day confinement for our criminal executives to that which would probably be affixed to a heroin addict who snatches a purse and empties its contents of, say, fourteen dollars! The point is this: the higher your income, the better protection you get from the entire legal system: lawyers, judges, jailkeepers, the rest of society.

17. For the story of Rockefeller and others of the same ilk, most of whom miraculously stayed out of jail, see the rollicking account by Matthew Josephson, *The Robber Barons* (Harcourt, Brace, 1936). For a more recent view, see Peter d'A. Jones, *The Robber Barons Revisited* (Lexington, Mass.: Heath, 1968).

18. This sordid tale is told in, among other places, Richard A. Smith, The Incredible Electrical Conspiracy," *Fortune*, April and May, 1961.

If your life of crime amounts to an occasional petty burglary and an even rarer mugging, you will probably be put away for ever-increasing amounts of time. If, on the other hand, you are guilty merely of being a monopolist whose only crime is living a life of luxury at the expense of all those who buy your products or work at your factories, you will not only avoid prosecution, you will be considered by many a paragon of diligence, good works, and morality. All this, in spite of the fact that laws with criminal provisions making it illegal to attempt to monopolize any industry (as the automobile industry has been monopolized) have been on the Federal books for more than eighty years.

Though these are but a few contrasting examples, they do shed light on the central issue that what kind of crime one commits is closely related to the income class one comes from, and that the harshness of the penalty for theft, for example, is determined less by the actual amount of money stolen than by the way in which the theft was committed. Moreover, as was mentioned earlier, criminals get distinctly different treatment by the legal system once they are indicted, and this difference also is closely related to their income class. For example, the ability of the rich to avoid the courts between indictment and conviction can be compared to the treatment given the poor in New York City who run afoul of the law. A New York City Council Subcommittee, commenting upon the city's jails, said: "Our present bail system constitutes a de facto system of preventive detention of the poor; the process by which a person is detained bears less relationship to considerations of justice or correction than to economic status. . . . More than 40% of the defendants are remanded to detention, not because they are likely to commit a crime or jump bail, but because they lack sufficient resources to post bond." [19] The same report indicated that in November, 1971, eight thousand men were being detained in New York City jails awaiting trial; this means, of course, that about thirty-two hundred of the city's inmates were there because they could not afford to buy their freedom. This kind of treatment before the law simply does not befall rich people in our society, and about this point there can be no real argument.

An insider's view of the issue should add an important final

19. *New York Times*, October 26, 1971, p. 30.

dimension to the argument. In providing his own evidence that poor people are treated unequally before the law, the late "Soledad Brother" George Jackson wrote:

> This is my eleventh year of being shoveled into every major prison in the most populous state in the nation—and the largest prison system in the world. . . . At each institution I've been in, 30 to sometimes 40 percent of those held are black, and *every one* of the many thousands I've encountered was from the working or lumpenproletariat class. There may be a few exceptions, but I simply have not met any of them in my eleven years. . . . I am confined now in San Quentin Prison . . . and all of [its] maximum security cells are filled—eleven of them with black men—every one of them without exception from the working class.[20]

And, to generalize his point, Jackson quoted Howard Moore, one of Angela Davis's attorneys:

> All black people, wherever they are, whatever their crimes, even crimes against other blacks, are political prisoners because the system has dealt with them differently than with whites. Whitey gets the benefit of every law . . . and the benefit of being judged by . . . other white people. Blacks don't get the benefit of any such jury trial by peers. Such a trial is almost a cinch to result in the conviction of a black person, and it's a conscious political decision that blacks don't have those benefits.

The argument that our state and national prison system is designed especially to keep unruly low-income elements out of the lives of the middle class is, to put it mildly, a controversial one; it is nonetheless the view of many people who have actually served time, and their unique perspective should be considered seriously.

The point is that being income-poor means getting relatively poor services from the omnipresent American legal system, which amounts to a further reduction in the real income of poor people. Of course, to be poor *and* black (or Puerto Rican, Mexican-American, or American Indian) is to get even fouler treatment before the law and thus have that much less real income.

20. George Jackson, "The Last Words of a Soledad Brother," *Esquire*, March, 1972, p. 111.

The Victims of Crime

There is still a further dimension to this matter of income classes and crime. Consider crimes of violence. To be poor is much more frequently to suffer the direct consequences of these crimes. In fact, the lower your income, and the darker your skin, the more likely you are to be the victim of a violent crime. Blacks, for example, are four times more likely to be robbed than whites; black women are four times more likely to be raped than white women. If you live in the core of a city of over one million, you are three times more likely to be the victim of an "index," or major, crime than if you live in a suburb of that city.[21] You are also more likely to be the victim of a business crime, since typically you will be less well prepared to defend yourself against the hucksters who fill the television screen and swarm over your doorstep with an unremitting bombardment of lies about their products. Many poor people are less educated and thus less sophisticated than others; they are frequently less able to distinguish between a good deal and a bad one, are more likely to be victimized by the fast operators who emerge from under the rocks of any social order, and are more easily hoodwinked into spending beyond their needs.[22] To be poor is to be more frequently victimized by crime if you are not a criminal and more often victimized by the law if you are one.

One could go on forever with this list of afflictions suffered by the American poor which do not emerge from simple statistical data on urban poverty. If you are poor, your garbage is picked up less frequently, your streets are dirtier, your house or apartment is less likely to be adequately maintained by the landlord, your neighborhood is more frequently next to an urban highway, your children have fewer parks to play in, you have more cars to dodge, vehicles, incidentally, more likely owned by oth-

21. This information is from *Report of the National Advisory Commission on Civil Disorders* (New York: Bantam, 1968). The *Report* will hereafter be referred to as the "Kerner Commission Report," after its director, Otto Kerner, who may be something of an expert on crime himself, having recently been indicted for fraud while holding public office in Illinois.

22. David Caplovitz, *The Poor Pay More* (New York: Free Press, 1967).

ers, since you will depend upon ill-financed, broken-down public transportation systems for most of your travel; [23] you will also have more pollution to inhale, more noise to suffer, fewer stores to shop at and higher prices to pay, more hostile police to deal with when you don't need them and fewer available when you do, less frequent vacations to enjoy, more crime, less health, more disease, and less education. Thus, to have a low income in America is also to receive poor services (such as the kinds mentioned here), and the result is that the difference between the absolute income of poor people and others is *much* greater than the Social Security Administration figures indicate.

Thomas Gladwin, an urban anthropologist, has written a powerful book on poverty, most of which discusses the non-monetary aspects of being poor (see my Acknowledgments). Several of his chapter headings, which follow here in verse form, adequately outline his book and neatly summarize all that I have tried to say on this matter:

> poverty is being poor
> poverty is being despised
> poverty is being incompetent
> poverty is being powerless

The "real" characteristics of poverty, therefore, are the noises, the smells, the fears and frustrations of living in a central city with a small income. The family with a ten-thousand-dollar income is not just twice as well off as the family with five thousand dollars—in fact, the difference may be that between the life and death of each of these families.

RELATIVE POVERTY

If, to this point, the evidence that statistical data on poverty are themselves quite poor has been unconvincing, let me add one

23. In 1970, almost 60 percent of all households with less than three thousand dollars income did not own an automobile: on the other hand, less than 5 percent of households with incomes of over ten thousand dollars were without automobiles, probably, in most cases, by choice. From U.S. Bureau of the Census, *Statistical Abstract of the United States: 1971*, 92nd ed. (Washington, D.C., 1971), p. 321.

last argument. We have been discussing "absolute" poverty—that is, the poverty of those whose income falls below some absolute, minimum amount, however calculated. One implication of these data is that if we increased the minimum, the data might be more meaningful, might give a truer idea of the number of people with less than "adequate" incomes. Perhaps so. However, there is an inherent disadvantage of using absolute income levels as an index, however high or low. That weakness stems from the fact that to some, poverty is simply not having as much as one's neighbor; this is called "relative" poverty.[24] Let me give you some data which will emphasize what this means.

If we look at income data broken down into income classes, we get the following figures for families in 1947 and 1969:[25]

Income Classes	Percentage of Total Income Received	
	1947	1969
Lowest Fifth	5.0	5.6
Second Lowest Fifth	11.8	12.3
Third Lowest Fifth	17.0	17.6
Second Highest Fifth	23.1	23.4
Highest Fifth	43.0	41.0
Top 5 percent	17.2	14.7

Below are the 1962 *wealth* holdings of the rich. (Wealth holdings are distinguished from income in that the former refer to one's stock of assets—land, bonds, stocks, real estate—while the latter refers to current flow of money income from these and other assets, such as rent, wages, and profits.) These wealth

24. For one such definition of relative poverty, see Victor Fuchs, "Redefining Poverty and Redistributing Income," *The Public Interest*, Summer, 1967. Fuchs defines poverty as income levels below one-half the median national income. In 1971, such a level would have been about forty-five hundred to five thousand dollars. Though I would certainly consider this kind of measurement an improvement over the SSA definition, it seems subject, nevertheless, to most of the criticisms in this chapter which I am applying to the SSA data.

25. These data and those in the following table are taken from Frank Ackerman *et al.*, "Income Distribution in the United States," *Review of Radical Political Economics*, Summer, 1971, pp. 22–25.

holdings are concentrated among the rich even *more* than is current income:

	Wealth Group		
	Top 20%	Top 5%	Top 1%
Total Wealth Owned	76%	50%	31%
Business and Professions	89%	62%	39%
Corporate Stock Owned	96%	83%	61%
Homes Owned	52%	19%	6%

It is important to note that these income relationships have not changed significantly since 1947, a twenty-five-year period during which so much has allegedly been done for the poor in this country. Families in the lowest one-fifth received 5.0 percent of the total income of Americans in 1947—about the same as they receive now—while the top 5 percent received about 17.2 percent. What has happened is that the top one-fifth has lost relatively to everyone *but* the poor. The point of this is that people in the lowest fifth income class are still just as poor, compared to everyone else, as they were in 1947. And thus, in relative terms, the number of poor has not changed at all since that time. It is important to think about these relative figures, for they are, in my judgment, the most important ones.

If you and your family earn four thousand dollars a year now, it may mean that, in absolute terms, you are *worse* off than you would have been with an equivalent amount in 1947, looking only at income figures which have been adjusted for inflation. This is an important point, because in trying to figure out what happened in the nineteen-sixties, many observers have taken these absolute figures and tried to show that the number of poor actually declined by millions of families. However, in our example, if you assume that urban services have clearly degenerated since 1947, and note the additional fact that mass television ownership makes it clear to *everyone* what *everyone else* is buying, having four thousand dollars in 1970 may give you a lower living standard, may be less satisfying, than having the equivalent amount in 1947. Look, however, at the following "over-

whelming" evidence that we are abolishing all kinds of poverty
in the United States (according to Federal census data):

Year	Number of Poor (in Millions)
1959	39.5
1963	36.4
1967	27.8
1968	25.4
1969	24.3

Data like these on *absolute* poverty are the cause of great sighs
of relief for most persons who read them, since they show that
over *one-third* of American poverty was abolished during the
nineteen-sixties. Especially disheartening is that the data provide all those who like to minimize the extent of the poverty
problem in our country with a convenient set of statistics with
which to undermine new antipoverty programs. I do hope that
the previous discussion makes one at least *suspect* that these
data tell us very little of any real value.

To sum up this discussion of poverty data, let me say that
trying to understand poverty only in terms of a simple figure on
absolute income levels is not to do much. Many of the more direct consequences of income poverty cannot be translated into
income figures, and this fact tends to obliterate any significant
value of Social Security poverty-income levels. Therefore, those
who throw these figures around, asking all comers to take them
as true or even rough measures of how many people are not adequately provided for in this social system, only fool themselves
and their unreflective readers. Urban poverty will continue to
exist as long as central cities are surrounded with suburbs where
the living is easier, healthier, cleaner, and safer; thus poverty is
simply one of the more obvious characteristics of a social order
which, for reasons we will spend some time on, doesn't provide
for its poorest citizens. Think of poverty as a *BIG* problem.
Think of it as a serious moral dilemma for a presumably civilized society. Think of poverty as one of the results of our own
privileged position in the world. Think of it as a personal trag-

edy to most of those who suffer it. Think about poverty in all these ways, *then* think about the statistics; they *may* tell you *something* worth knowing.

II. *The Causes of Urban Poverty*

THE THEORY OF THE UNHEAVENLY POOR

There are quite obviously any number of explanations about why people in the city are poor, however many poor there may be. These explanations range from an absolute condemnation of the poor themselves—they are shiftless, they are lazy, they are dishonest, they are untrustworthy—to an absolute condemnation of the U.S. industrial, capitalist system—it doesn't work for everyone, wasn't designed to do so, never will do so, and so on.

Somewhere between these two positions lie *most* of the explanations, but not necessarily the true one. Most academics who have tried to explain these matters are, by nature and training, not extremist; thus their theories are generally somewhere between the two polar cases. We can begin with what might be called the "simple-minded" theory of urban poverty, the outlines of which were suggested above. According to this theory, probably the explanation given by most Americans, the poor are poor because, from their point of view, it is easier to be without income than to do the work necessary to get it. This bootstrap theory, of course, views an individual's income as the reward of individual merit and dismisses as irrelevant such personal characteristics as age, education, family income, sex, race, region of the country, health, and all the other very obvious factors that help determine the flow of income to an individual or to a family. Such a theory as this would suggest that, for example, David Rockefeller's $600 million wealth (or whatever) reflects his natural abilities and his rugged determination rather than his family background. The simple-minded thesis would also explain the poverty of the Appalachian white, now in Chicago, whose coal-mining skills are not needed there, or anywhere, as being determined largely by his unwillingness to accept the going wage-rate for available jobs. What's wrong with this simple but

popular theory of urban poverty is that it doesn't explain anything; it is a mere tautology, whereby one's income is assumed
to be a measure of one's capacity for making income, which is
assumed to be measured by one's income. It can, I believe, be
dismissed.

More persuasive than the crude theory outlined above is the
much more sophisticated but quite similar theory of poverty expressed by the political scientist Edward Banfield in his now
widely read book *The Unheavenly City*.[26] Because this book has
apparently had such considerable influence, even on presidents,[27] it is worth some discussion here and will also be taken
up at several points in later chapters. Banfield's argument about
urban poverty is more detailed, more specifically related to the
urban context, and more interesting than the "simple-minded"
theory. He explains urban poverty as the end result of what he
calls "the logic of metropolitan development." The urban poor,
disproportionately black and rural migrants, have, like all their
counterparts, come to the city, which offers them only a place in
line; no quick success, but presumably better opportunity than
the marginal rural economy most originally migrated from.
Many of these urban poor, Banfield argues, have brought with
them decidedly lower-class behavior patterns, which are passed
on to their children, and which are inconsistent with the labor
markets in urban areas and the polite sensibilities of the urban-
ites already on the scene. While not going into very great detail
about what *caused* these lower-class habits, Banfield discusses at
length, and with great enthusiasm, the habits themselves. He describes with abandon the various kinds of shiftlessness of the
urban poor, and argues finally that they will end their poverty
only when they change their habits into something other than
lower-class ones.

Banfield's presentation is impressive and persuasive, but his

26. Edward Banfield, *The Unheavenly City* (Boston: Little, Brown,
1970).
27. Banfield is relatively close to the Nixon Administration. Among other
capacities, he has served as chairman of the Presidential Task Force on
Model Cities in 1970. In any case, if one reads Banfield's book and reads
about Nixon's "city program," one can easily understand why they apparently listen to each other on the subject of what to do about social problems.

argument shares with the earlier "simple-minded" one a failure to explain much about the causes of poverty. He argues that lower-class people in the city are poor because they do not "make preparation for the future," which, in essence, is the principal characteristic of what he calls lower-class behavior. So a significant number of low-income people are poor because they are lower-class; however, Banfield has not developed an independent way to verify when a person is "living for the present" except to note that many of those who are poor *must* be doing so. As a consequence, his argument, as far as I can tell, does not explain much about why there are lower classes (and why there are poor), except that blacks who came from the South and other rural migrants didn't have the necessary skills to compete in urban labor markets.

The main problem with most of Banfield's argument, therefore, is that it doesn't tell us anything 1) which is not obvious to all but the most inexperienced, or 2) which is not simply a value judgment on his part. For example, his suggestion that urban blacks frequently display "lower-class habits," using his definition, is something that everyone knows, though other observers have used different characteristics to show how and try to explain why the black poor often act differently from middle-class people. However, his argument that nothing significant can be done about these habits through private or public income subsidies is only a judgment on his part, unfortunate in this case because he 1) cannot prove such a claim, and 2), more important, because many people have read his book and believed him, assuming that like all good scholars he was dealing only with the "facts of the matter." God forbid!

There can be no doubt, however, about the accuracy of Banfield's description of the behavior of *some* of the urban poor. The inability to stay on the job, keep regular hours, submit to discipline, stick with training programs—all these and other, similar characteristics have plagued attempts to get and keep in the labor force many lower-income urban people. However, this merely describes their outward behavior without giving any explanation of—or in Banfield's case much sympathy for—how such habits are developed, and whether the external characteristics of lower-class behavior accurately reflect the hidden, more powerful reasons why poor people view the urban labor market with a great deal of fear, suspicion, and hostility. It seems clear, at least to me, that we need to go elsewhere to discover the larger causes of urban poverty. Banfield is too sure of himself, too indifferent to considerable data from sources at odds with his own thesis, and too obviously hostile toward the lower classes whose behavior he is trying to explain.[28]

ECONOMETRIC THEORIES OF POVERTY

At another level of abstraction is the work of econometricians, or "economic statisticians." One of the best-known econometricians is Lester Thurow, and his best-known work is *Poverty and Discrimination*.[29] In trying to explain the economic aspects of racial discrimination, Thurow has constructed a theory of poverty which has tested rather well against the observed numerical data on poverty. Thurow begins his analysis with the economist's theory of marginal product, which, in essence, explains the flow of income to an individual as determined by that individual's productivity in labor markets. The implication of such models is that an individual's holding of human capital— his/her training and educational experience—determines, in large part, his/her income. Thurow has expanded on the "human capital" theme and has tried to measure a number of additional variables which obviously determine income flow. His model goes something like this: Let us hypothesize that the number of poor in a particular state depends (especially) upon the following variables:

1. number of people in the state living on farms;
2. number of families headed by a black person (as a measure of the extent to which poverty is caused by discrimination);
3. number of high-wage industries in the state;
4. number of families headed by someone working full-time;

28. It is not necessary here to take my word about the limitations of many aspects of Banfield's argument. Most of the reviews of the book by academics in the field were quite negative; some were even hostile. See, for example, Richard Senett's review in *New York Review of Books,* August 13, 1970.

29. Lester Thurow, *Poverty and Discrimination* (Washington, D.C.: Brookings Institution, 1969).

5. number of family heads with less than eight years of education.

Though there are other variables in his model, these are the most important ones. (I shall go into greater detail about how econometricians do their work in Chapter 3.) After testing his model statistically, Thurow found, for example, that:

1. city people are less likely to be poor than farmers;

2. people with an education of less than eight years are likely to make significantly less income than others;

3. the health of the area economy is especially important as a determinant of income flow to the poor, because they are the first to be laid off, the last to be hired;

4. poor people are more likely than not to be geographically located closer to less productive, low-wage industries, especially highly competitive ones; and

5. all other things remaining the same, blacks tend to make less adequate incomes than whites.

These statistical conclusions, of course, are all consistent with a commonsense explanation of poverty and do not vary much from one econometrician to the other. What the econometrician seeks to do is to give some precision to the measurements. Thus Thurow argues that, for example, a 1 percent *increase* in the number of poor family heads educated beyond the eighth grade will lead to a 0.43 percent *decrease* in the number of poor people. There is, I suppose, some merit in these models, given faith in the data on which they are based, and faith in the statistical methods which make them possible.[30]

The main shortcoming of the econometric method, however, is that it fails utterly to explain the *causes* of poverty in a very important sense. To hypothesize that a black man, with six years of education, living in a low-wage industrial area, just off the farm, is likely to be poor, and then to test that hypothesis against observed data, is only to give precision to the obvious. Such an approach still doesn't tell us why the important varia-

30. For an excellent brief discussion of these matters, see Robert Hinckley, "Some Comments on Economic Methodology" (mimeographed, available on request from Charles Sackrey, Smith College, Northampton, Mass.). Also useful in this context is Oskar Morgenstern, *On the Accuracy of Economic Observations*, 2nd ed. (Princeton: Princeton University Press, 1963).

bles are what they are. It doesn't tell, for example, why a bright man with eight years' education will get a job *after* a dull man with a high-school degree; why a black man gets less income for the *same* job than does a white man. It doesn't tell us either why a farmer working for twelve hours a day at hard physical labor makes less than a stockbroker who spends his time sitting in a comfortable office, wheeling and dealing in the stocks of American corporations. It fails to explain why blacks and the other latest migrants to the urban core fail so utterly to get jobs in high-paying firms which have job openings many unemployed blacks could fill. This method of studying urban poverty also fails to explain why the world's wealthiest economy must always keep a quarter or so of its citizens at the bottom, a bottom devoid of ample opportunity for those most in need of it.

What I mean is this: Thurow's model, and similar ones, gives precision, or tries to give precision, to a view of the urban labor market and of income flow to urban families that is based upon *marginal* changes in the existing scheme of things. Thurow explains what happens in the labor market but takes as given the basic features of that labor market and the larger social institutions in which that market functions.

RADICAL THEORIES OF POVERTY [31]

The inadequacies of all such theories of poverty have been aptly summarized by Howard Wachtel. He argues:

> Social science research has mirrored our social ideology. Virtually all the past and contemporary social science research has concentrated on the characteristics of individuals who are defined

31. What follows here defines as radicals those economists who believe that poverty cannot be eliminated in an advanced capitalist country. I have called them "radical" because this is what they call themselves. Other social scientists, such as urban anthropologists Eleanor Leacock, Thomas Gladwin, and Charles Valentine (see discussion in Chapter 2), and sociologist Lee Rainwater ("The American Underclass: Comment," *Trans-Action*, February, 1969, p. 9), have come to similar conclusions about the plight of the poor in our social system. Whether they think of themselves as radical or not, I do not know. I do believe, however, that an insistence that poverty is a fault of the capitalist system seriously questions the value of liberal reform as a way to end it. The discussion in Chapter 3 will return to this issue.

as poor by the federal government. Being poor is associated with a set of individual characteristics: sex, age, race, education, marital status, etc. But these are not *causes* of poverty. There have been dozens of studies of so-called causes of poverty; not surprisingly, these studies merely associate the cause of poverty with a particular set of individual characteristics. For example, if you are poor and have low levels of education, it does not necessarily follow that low levels of education are a cause of poverty since education itself is endogenous to the system. The causes of inequality in education and their impact on incomes must be analyzed by examining social class, the role of the state, and the way in which educational markets function.

There has been essentially no social science research in the last 10 years on the question of poverty which has gone beyond a mere cataloging of the characteristics of the poor. A proper formulation of the problem would start with poverty as a result of the normal functioning of the societal institutions in a capitalist economy. . . .[32]

Let me clarify what I think Wachtel means with a few simple examples. To observe that women have lower incomes than men who do the same job is not to say that a woman's sex is the cause of her lower income, except insofar as you accept as given

32. Howard Wachtel, "Looking at Poverty from a Radical Perspective," *Review of Radical Political Economics*, Summer, 1971, p. 2. Professor Wachtel, and several other young American economists, have recently established a group called the Union of Radical Political Economists (URPE). The group publishes a quarterly, *The Review of Radical Political Economics*, and occasional papers, and meets frequently in various metropolitan areas to discuss ideas and politics, and to supply each other with job information. URPE is, in principle, aimed at directing the research and political efforts of the American economics profession away from its emphasis on sterile, mathematical scientism to a more relevant, interdisciplinary, and political approach to the United States economic order. Also, the typical radical economist is convinced that American capitalism is not a desirable long-range solution to our economic needs. Thus, many radical economists are Marxists or adopt similar anticapitalist ideological positions. I have used the term "radical" in this book to describe the kind of methodological and substantive analysis that these (mostly) young economists are currently engaged in. I use the term "revolutionary" here to describe political action aimed at an eventual replacement of the existing order with something else. In other words, one can be a radical economist (for example, a research economist) and not be a revolutionary (which assumes some kind of political activity). I have defined these terms here because they are both used in contemporary parlance with such a great variety of meanings, and because this distinction between them is assumed throughout the rest of the book.

the whole past history of the human race and its failure to grant equal opportunity for women to participate in the labor market. Her womanness is the cause of her lower income, given a social system which has forced her into jobs which are defined as relatively unproductive. Similarly, the poverty of an American Indian —and more than two-thirds are statistically poor—cannot be "explained" by the Indian's lack of education, unless that one assumes as given the social system which confined him to a marginal reservation and the historical causes of that confinement.

The point is that behind all these superficial theories of poverty is a social system based upon certain principles, one of the results of which is that millions of people in the cities are poor. And, in this larger framework, the cause of urban poverty is the *entire social system,* a set of social habits which make it difficult, no matter what courage, no matter what perseverance a hypothetical urban black woman may have, for her to get out of poverty. This explanation of poverty as the fault of the system rather than the fault of the individual is, of course, the basis of many theories of poverty quite at odds with those of Banfield, Thurow, and most other academic social scientists. These alternative, more radical theories of poverty are worth mention, and for those who have trafficked over the years in Marxist—or other anticapitalist—analyses the basic framework of what follows will come as no surprise. Radical social scientists in this country are probably more in agreement on the idea that the state in an advanced capitalist society serves the needs of its population in direct proportion to the income they receive than they are on any other issue. A simple, though typical, exposition of this notion follows.

Consider an abstract model that goes something like this: assuming a capitalist system, we divide the adult population into two sectors: the capitalists and the workers.[33] The capitalists will receive for their efforts something called property income

33. This kind of model will quickly be recognized as Marxian, and the use of this example is not by chance. As I indicated in the previous note, a great number of radical economists—probably most of them—are either Marxists, in their own terms, or are sympathetic to Marxian methodology, with its insistence on scope and interdisciplinary studies.

—rent, profit, interest—and the workers will receive wages and salaries. Also, because the capitalists own the machines, they will receive the biggest payoff from the operation of the machines. (So far, this theory is consistent with reality, in which the overwhelming majority of the American rich are rich because they receive rent, interest, or profits—or a combination of the three.) The poor in such a society will most likely be working-class, because by definition they do not have access to capital. In addition, those with the largest incomes—the capitalists —will control the state, that is, the functions of government at all levels. Then, since the capitalists write the laws, they will write them so as to benefit themselves the most. They will also, because of their economic and political power, control the means of communication: the newspapers, the radio and television networks, the printing presses—all those forms of communication which are assumed in radical models to determine importantly the social values of the participants in the social system.

Moreover, the capitalists will guarantee the entrance of their own children into the upper class by developing an educational system which stratifies the class structure by providing educational facilities and funds to students in direct proportion to the income of their parents. The teachers and administrators in such an educational system will spend no small effort in convincing students from the lower-income classes to accept the fact of what Peter Schrag has called "their second-class citizenship." That is, the lack of self-confidence that so many social scientists have observed in the behavior of lower-class people will be carefully nurtured by the educational system in a capitalist society.

Among the most important values determined by these economic and educational institutions in a capitalist society are those associated with the proper recompense for different kinds of labor. Therefore, not surprisingly, the capitalists, who control these things, will define an adequate income for themselves as distinctly higher than an adequate income for workers, no matter how crude, selfish, or greedy the capitalists' efforts are which lead to the income. And further, if the capitalists, or those in control of the legislatures and the newspapers, see fit to define one particular race, or one of the sexes, or certain foreigners as inferior to the rest, there arise in labor markets certain jobs which are held in safekeeping for those inferiors to fill. There will arise "colored jobs," "women's work," and other categories of labor for which a relative pittance will be paid, for it is accepted by the public—whose ideas are shaped by the flow of communication from the capitalist press and TV—that such jobs are not worthy of higher incomes. How else, except through this kind of analysis, can one explain the fact that I, a professor, who spend my time in no apparent service to the cause of increasing the GNP, am paid about the same amount as the plumber who keeps the sewage from backing up and swallowing us all? My salary reflects certain prejudices about my status in society, my role in keeping it all going, and, above all, an artificially restricted labor supply.

Similarly, how does one explain the $800,000 paid annually to the head of General Motors for leading the corporation whose products are helping to ruin our cities and countryside, as compared to the $4,000 paid to the public employee who cleans up the cities' debris? It must be explained in terms of some power acquired by the head of GM that enables him to get that much income, at the expense of all those to whom the income would flow if he didn't get it.

The radical analyst would go beyond this basic introduction to a more complete explanation of why wages in this society for all kinds of work reflect a good deal more than just the supply and demand for workers in existing markets. Take the football player, for example, who is paid fifty thousand dollars annually because he can kick a football farther and straighter than anyone on earth. An orthodox economist would explain this wage in terms of the demand for that player's services, measured by the number of fans who come out to see him, and the supply of people who can kick a ball that far. Since the demand is great and the supply highly restricted, he makes a high wage. However, all this does not explain, or identify the cause of, his wage, unless one accepts as given all those other social institutions which legitimize the football player's behavior and the way he is paid for it. Such a wage assumes a set of tax laws which allow it to exist, and tax laws in this country clearly reflect the needs of the rich. (There are more tax loopholes for oil millionaires than there are for unemployed Puerto Rican laundry workers, and the reasons for them are not hard to determine.) [34] Such a wage also assumes an essentially private ownership and control of professional football, though in many societies such efforts are organized more along the lines of the general welfare than exclusively on the basis of the welfare of the athletes and their owners. Further, the player's wage reflects a subsidy paid to the club owner by the local citizenry, who most likely financed the purchase of the stadium he plays in, a citizenry that purchase organized violence rather than purchasing other commodities. The point is that there is nothing sacrosanct about the player's wage. It measures his productivity and worth only *in terms of the way the society is organized*. Change the laws, change the customs, change the habits and you change his wage rate, and all the wage rates of everyone else.

In this kind of analysis, therefore, poverty is nothing more than the condition of those whose efforts have been described as worthless by those who make the rules. We could pass a law today which would take all the *property* income (in the form of rent, interest, stockholder profits, and capital gains) from the rich, for which most presently *do nothing*, and give it to the unemployed poor, who also presently do nothing, and, hypothetically, total output would remain the same.

The point is that the radical takes an entirely different view of the whole issue of urban poverty. The radical theory of poverty is a theory of the economic system—its ownership and control, its relationship to the state, its past history, its present system of legitimizing myths. In the radical's view, the old woman living in low-income housing, who feeds herself and her three

34. I heard on the radio a recent news report that the Internal Revenue Service will investigate the tax records of a few individuals in this country who made over $200,000 in a single year but who paid *no* Federal income taxes. This kind of exemption is ordinarily provided only for those families with less than $4,000 in income. If there is any doubt that wealthy people get special treatment from Federal tax laws, read, at random, in the Federal Tax Code. For example, if I receive $500,000 in income from state bonds (all of which are owned by the richest 1 percent of the nation's families) I will pay *no* Federal taxes on this income. If, on the other hand, I receive $10,000 in wages from a factory job, and have a wife and three children, I will pay about $800 in Federal taxes. So much for equity.

motherless grandchildren with wages from working in a laundry, though she is paid less income, is not necessarily less productive than her suave young landlord, whisking around town in a sportscar purchased by the rents paid him by poor people. The fact that he is paid more than she is but one result of a quaint and unfortunate social custom regarding money payments for services rendered in the economy.

In general, there are a host of conflicting explanations of poverty, ranging from the view that it is an inevitable and irremedial consequence of "lower-class behavior" to the radical explanation that poverty is a necessary result of industrial capitalism. What is most important here about this great variety of theories is that each carries with it implications for particular kinds of social policy. And it is this dimension of any "economic theory of poverty" which demands that the theoretician come to terms with the policy implied by his model. Thus the "pure economics" of the typical contemporary economist, because it implies certain political responses, means that a more complete discussion of urban poverty—or of any other social problem— becomes a problem in *political* economy. This result is an important byproduct of modern social analysis and cannot be avoided, in my judgment, by the usual protestation from economic "scientists" that their job is complete once they have described a problem and hypothesized about its causes.

I shall take up the issue of political responses to varying theories of urban poverty in Chapter 4; now, however, it is necessary to discuss in greater detail two questions: 1) what are the special characteristics of urban *black* poverty? and, 2) what special insights into this problem can be provided by those of us who pose as economists—that is, scientists in quest of the nature and meaning of the social order? I have argued in Chapter 1 that urban black poverty is an especially serious aspect of the "urban problem." The next chapter attempts to justify that claim. In addition, Chapter 2 elaborates the differences between "liberal" and "radical" theories of poverty by adding certain details to each argument which have been developed especially for the purpose of relating American poverty to the racial biases of the American people.

Chapter Two

THE POVERTY OF
URBAN BLACK PEOPLE

In October, 1971, the *New York Times* published new census data showing that the average income of Spanish-speaking Americans (including Chicanos, Cuban immigrants, and Puerto Ricans) was higher than that of black Americans, even though there are, proportionately, many more Spanish-speaking Americans with *less* than five years of education than there are blacks. In 1971, men of Spanish origin made, on the average, about 76 percent of white male incomes, while black men made about 61 percent of white male incomes.[1]

As a consequence of this evidence (and a great deal of other evidence like it), which has convinced me beyond serious doubt that black Americans suffer greater discrimination than *any* other ethnic minority in America, I decided, when planning this book, to concentrate on urban black poverty, rather than on all urban poverty. The poverty of urban blacks is more severe than that of others in the cities, though evidence indicates that among the Spanish-speaking group, Puerto Ricans, on the aver-

1. *New York Times*, October 18, 1971, p. 1.

age, may even fare worse than blacks. It is my judgment, nonetheless, that black poverty is different enough in both scope and
intensity to justify special consideration. Besides, all that is said
here about the problems of the black poor applies to all the
urban poor, to one degree or the other.[2] In essence, it simply applies *especially* well to black people.

At the outset, I think it is legitimate to question my ability to
make any meaningful sense out of the problems of the black
poor since I have never been poor, nor have I had the experience of being anything other than a rather typical American
WASP. I recognize the enormous limitations of discussing an aspect of life which one has not experienced, even remotely. And
what can an ex-southerner-upper-middle-class-WASP-professor
say about the poverty of urban blacks, anyway? Among all the
other problems of social science, this one stands out as especially severe. To try to describe and analyze a world one *is* part
of is an inherent limitation of social theory; on the other hand, it
is alleged by many that to attempt descriptions of parts of reality which one is *not* a part of is even *more* difficult. Black students and faculty across the nation have indicated their own
suspicion of white interpretations of black history and black
problems by establishing, where possible, their own academic
programs, which ideally they administer and operate themselves. I'm aware of all this, and more. And, as a consequence, I
would invite everyone to be suspicious of my explanations of
black poverty. I am trying to describe a part of the larger social
order in which I live, but it is also a part which I have never experienced. I am, as it were, doubly afflicted. Others are too, as it
turns out.

Reading, for example, articles by Harvard's John Kain, a
white economist generally considered one of the more formida-
ble "experts" on urban affairs, and Peter Labrie, a black pro-

2. For excellent discussions of the urban poverty of those other than
blacks, see Dick Wakefield's moving essay on Puerto Ricans in New York
City, *Island in the City* (New York: Corinth, 1957); and Oscar Lewis's
work, mentioned in Chapter 1. See also the excellent book on the poverty
of recent white migrants from the south in Chicago by Todd Gitlin and
Nanci Hollander, *Uptown: Poor Whites in Chicago* (New York: Harper &
Row, 1970).

fessor at the University of California, clearly reveals that a white man and a black man can analyze identical data concerning the principal characteristics of black urban ghettos and from them develop entirely different descriptions of reality with entirely different implications for social policy.[3] Since much of the writing of white academics concerning blacks is influenced by a combination of guilt, latent hostility, misunderstanding, and a reactionary paradigm, it is no wonder that when blacks study the same data, they reach different conclusions. Indeed, a good part of the writing of blacks about their own problems is weakened by explicit or tacit theories of conspiracy and overblown visions of white racism. As a consequence, such works frequently degenerate into unsubstantiated rhetoric revealing little more than the prejudices of the writers. My point is this: the current and past literature on black problems, in the city and elsewhere, is a veritable garden of misinformation, an enormous library filled mostly with charges and countercharges; a mixed bag of analysis and polemics. And, most surely, my observations on the matter reflect elements of all these limitations, plus some which are singularly my own. Thus, for good or bad, what follows is what makes sense to me, and is hopefully not seriously impaired by the methodological problems that stand between my mind and an understanding of black poverty.

My plan is this: *first,* I will briefly review the migration patterns which since the turn of the century have resulted in the enormous immigration of southern blacks into American cities. The purpose here will be to provide evidence supporting the argument that today's city problems have been exported from the farms; *second,* I will describe present black segregation patterns in American cities which have followed upon black migration to the cities; *third,* I will describe briefly the larger dimensions of urban black poverty, providing data which are only impressionistic but which are indicative of the scope of the problem.

3. Compare Kain's article (with Joseph Persky) "Alternatives to the Gilded Ghetto," *The Public Interest,* Winter, 1969, pp. 74–87, to Labrie's "Black Central Cities: Dispersal or Rebuilding Parts 1 and 2," *Review of Black Political Economy,* vol. 1, nos. 2 and 3 (1971).

Following this descriptive part, I will survey the two most important kinds of theoretical explanations given for the concentration of poor blacks in central cities. These explanations are quite consistent with the discussion in the previous chapter suggesting that theories of urban poverty can be divided into 1) those which assume the *basic* features of American industrial capitalism as given and unchangeable, and 2) those which assume poverty as a necessary corollary of that system and for that reason advocate that the system be replaced.

I. The Northern Migration of Rural Black People

With regard to the migration of southern blacks, the facts of the matter can be summarized rather briefly.[4] The Negroes' migration to the North began on a large scale during World War I, as the opportunities offered by war industries provided many new opportunities for employment in the cities. And this migration continued in the twenties, because of the prosperity of that decade and because the excitement and glamor of the roaring twenties was, in the public mind, anyway, primarily confined to the large metropolitan areas. Though the depression in the thirties somewhat slowed black migration, between 1910 and 1940 about 1.55 million blacks had moved northward and were living in northern cities.

This pre–World War II migration, of course, laid the groundwork for the eventual urban segregation patterns and provided an indication of what might happen with even larger migrations. Blacks typically moved to the low-income, poor-housing districts in the central cities, mainly because their low income, plus discrimination in housing markets, forced them to choose between various kinds of cheap, crowded housing, and because of the proximity to relatives, friends, and potential job opportunities. And, probably, the problems these blacks experienced were not substantively different from those experienced now, as

4. Most of the data in this section are taken from Federal census findings and the *New York Times*; for a good overview of these migration patterns, see Charles Tilly, "Race and Migration to the American City," in James Q. Wilson, ed., *The Metropolitan Enigma* (Garden City: Doubleday, 1970), pp. 144–169; and Richard Sherman, ed., *The Negro and the City* (Englewood Cliffs: Prentice-Hall, 1970).

writers like Richard Wright, James Baldwin, Malcolm X, Ralph Ellison, and Claude Brown have pointed out. These men and others have written powerfully about their experiences while living in cities during the 1930–1960 period.

What was different about their experiences, compared to the current situation, was that the sheer number of blacks living in urban ghettos was then a good deal smaller than now. In addition, the gradual collapse in the flow of public services in urban areas, the congestion caused by increasing autos and decreasing public transportation, and all the rest had not yet become as severe a problem as it presently is, and, probably more important, the plight of urban blacks had simply not become a public issue. The problems of urban blacks during the fifties and before were severe, but they did not become a "crisis" in the public mind until the full effects of migration patterns after 1940 had worked themselves out in the late fifties and 1960's.

Of course, World War II provided another great range of opportunities for blacks in northern cities, and the migration continued, indeed at a much greater pace than ever before. Moreover, following the war, before migration patterns could return to prewar levels, there occurred in southern agricultural technology a series of developments which made obsolete a significant proportion of unskilled jobs in rural areas, a disproportionate number of which had been held by black people. However, the speed of this transformation from a rural to an industrial economy increased significantly between 1945 and 1950. For example, machine harvesting of cotton and corn was introduced on a large scale in 1950, and an important increase in soybean acreage (which demands little unskilled labor) further decreased the need for agricultural labor. Between 1949 and 1952, the need for unskilled labor in twenty Mississippi counties fell by 72 percent, and five years later it was down to 10 percent of the 1949 level.[5] Indeed, between 1940

5. These figures and much of the general framework of my argument here have been taken from Daniel Fusfeld, "The Basic Economics of the Urban and Racial Crisis," *Conference Papers of the Union for Radical Political Economics*, December, 1968, pp. 55–84. He suggests that the best account of how southern black workers were pushed out of agriculture is R. H. Day, "The Economics of Technological Change and the Demise of the Sharecropper," *American Economic Review*, June, 1967, pp. 427–449.

42   The Political Economy of Urban Poverty

and 1960, the number of man-hours needed for agricultural labor in Alabama, Louisiana, and Mississippi fell from an index of 247 percent to 93 percent (that is, to fell to about 40 percent of the 1940 level).[6]

The structural changes in southern agriculture in the late forties and early fifties sent forth new, unprecedented numbers of black migrants from the South to the North. In the 1940's, about 1.6 million blacks moved northward, more than had moved during the previous thirty years; in the 1950's still another 1.5 million moved North. Apparently because opportunities in the northern cities still compared favorably with those in the South, during the 1960's another 1.4 million blacks moved northward. Furthermore, the latest Census Bureau prediction is that this trend will continue throughout the present decade.

To complete the scenario, it should be pointed out that whites have been moving out of northern central cities as blacks move in. As an example of what has happened in the typical heavily populated, industrial city outside the South, consider migration patterns in New York City. During the 1960's, the white population (excluding Puerto Ricans) in New York City *decreased* by 986,000, while the number of black people in the city *increased* by 580,000.[7] The concentration of blacks in central cities all over the nation is clearly indicated by 1970 census data which show that while 23.3 percent of the population of the central cities of the nation's largest metropolitan areas are black people, only 4.5 percent of the suburbs are black. While the census data also indicate that there may have been some suburbanization of blacks in the 1960's, the data have not yet been analyzed adequately to determine whether this movement has been "salt and pepper" integration in outlying suburbs, or simply outward expansion from the core to the inner ring, where blacks have taken over neighborhoods earlier occupied by low-income whites.[8]

6. Day, p. 427.
7. *New York Times,* March 6, 1972, p. 72.
8. For an early, probably premature, evaluation of the data which suggest there has been "real" suburbanization of blacks in the 1960's, see David Birch, *The Economic Future of the City and Suburb* (New York: Committee on Economic Development, 1970), Report no. 30.

One final piece of evidence from the 1970 census data is worth noting: though these migrations have been heavy since 1940, more than half the American black population still lives in the South. This is the main reason why it is expected that the migrations will continue into the seventies, and it further explains why many economists have suggested that an important part of any urban antipoverty program would include efforts to stem the migration from the South by initiating rural antipoverty programs.

We have discussed earlier how the segregation patterns in central cities show that the migrant blacks have, for the most part, settled in the core areas of large metropolitan areas. The famous studies by sociologists Charles and Alma Taeuber,[9] and others, have shown that, in fact, in the typical American city in 1960, 85 percent or more of all blacks would have to move to different neighborhoods in order for the city to be "integrated." Apparently this pattern has not changed significantly since that year: a Census Bureau study in the mid-sixties showed that ". . . in most of the 12 large cities where special censuses were taken . . . the proportion of Negroes living in neighborhoods of greatest Negro concentration had increased since 1960." [10] And a more recent analysis of census data in New York shows that during the 1960's "the old segregated housing pattern was intensified," and that in 1970 more than two-thirds of the city's census tracts were either 90 percent white or 90 percent black.[11]

It should not be surprising that the incidence of poverty among these urban blacks is quite high, indeed higher than among any other ethnic or minority group in the country (with the exception of American Indians). The incidence of poverty among urban blacks would be expected, given the nature of the urban economy, and given the racial views of many whites who live in metropolitan areas. The earlier black migrants were typically low-skilled and from rural backgrounds, and they moved into the city to replace, in the urban labor markets, those low-

9. *Negroes in Cities: Residential Segregation and Neighborhood Change* (Chicago: Aldine, 1965).

10. Kerner Commission Report, p. 247.

11. *New York Times*, March 6, 1972, p. 1.

skilled whites who were following better job opportunities in
the suburbs.

All the economic consequences of the migration of blacks to
central cities, and the outmigration of industry and opportunity
to the suburbs, have been detailed in innumerable books and articles.[12] A crucial variable, of course, was the fact that white
employers since the end of World War II had quickened their
pace in taking their families and their firms to the suburbs. In
doing so they took with them an increasing number of jobs,
leaving the central-city economy even more dominated by two
kinds of employment opportunities: professional and clerical
jobs which have traditionally been inaccessible to blacks, and
low-paying service jobs: janitors, elevator operators, domestics.
As the number of blacks coming from the South grew each year,
the available jobs were decreasing in the central-city economy
on which most were absolutely dependent. Also, black workers
were made to suffer the consequences of what some economists
have called the "dual labor market." This matter is worth some
elaboration.

Alongside the great industrial firms in the U.S. economy, there
exists the so-called "competitive" sector. This group of firms is
characterized chiefly by a labor-intensive production process, by
fierce price competition with their rivals, and by relatively low
profit rates. Such a low-profit, competitive milieu is associated,
in general, with relatively low wage rates, and the employees in
these "marginal industries" are most typically low-skilled
and/or without credentials for higher-paying jobs. Of course,
such firms are precisely the kinds which would have job opportunities for low-skilled blacks recently migrated from the farm,
and accordingly the migrants, when they could find work, invariably had jobs in highly competitive, low-profit firms. (We will
take up this "marginal industry" concept again in Chapter 4.)

12. For a beginner, John Kain's little anthology *Race and Poverty: The
Economics of Discrimination* (Englewood Cliffs: Prentice-Hall, 1969) is excellent. It has a fair bibliography. Kain has done a great deal of the work
in gathering data to show what has happened to the movements of jobs
and people and what changes have occurred in urban housing markets during the past two decades. More about Kain's work is included in a later
footnote.

Moreover, for the black migrants, there was an additional problem associated with working in urban labor markets, and this was their race. As many studies have indicated, the marginal industries themselves—as well as all others—*also* possess a certain duality. This characteristic of an urban labor market derives primarily from the fact that public and private employment agencies, unions, and employers have quite simply reserved certain jobs for black people, and they are typically the lowest-paying ones. One study of the dual labor market in Chicago was summarized as follows:

> Segregation in the Northern labor market has been as efficient a mechanism for subjugating Negroes to second-class status as segregation in housing and education. In Chicago the process of allocating jobs to white workers is so effectively separated from the process of allocating jobs to Negro workers that year after year the differentials between white and Negro workers are maintained. At the same time, a large segment of the Negro labor force is relegated to the role of an urban peasantry destined to live off welfare payments and white paternalism. The Negro labor force, unlike those of other large ethnic groups, has not been allowed to assimilate into the metropolitan labor market. One hundred years after emancipation and forty-five years after urbanization, Negroes in Chicago are still systematically restricted in both the skills they may acquire and the extent to which they can utilize any given level of skills.[13]

Therefore, blacks who came to the city from the South were able to get only the lowest-paying jobs at the bottom of a labor market which punished them both for their blackness and for their relative lack of skills.

To compound their problems in relation to the labor market, there occurred among urban blacks a relatively large growth in population, since most of the migrants were from childbearing age groups. Coming from rural areas, they had a tendency to have large families, and since the infant mortality rate in north-

13. Harold Baron and Bennett Hymer, "The Dynamics of the Dual Labor Market," in David Gordon, ed., *Problems in Political Economy: An Urban Perspective* (Lexington, Mass.: Heath, 1971), p. 100. See also Michael Piore, "The Dual Labor Market: Theory and Implications," in Gordon, pp. 90–94.

ern cities was relatively small compared to that of the farm areas, the black urban population grew about 50 percent faster in the 1960's than the white population. Among other poverty-related results of this population growth among the migrants is the disproportionate increase in the number of young black males aged fourteen to twenty-four, who, in *any* population, are inclined to have a higher unemployment rate and a greater tendency to commit street crimes. So, in the 1970's our central cities have become increasingly black, and the incidence of poverty among these blacks exceeds that of any other large urban group. Let me review some of the poverty data which compare black poverty to that of urban whites.

II. Some Data on Urban Black Poverty

Earlier I argued that absolute figures on poverty should be used with considerable care, and that relative figures were superior ones. Let me concentrate on the latter for a minute and in so doing try to indicate that however serious the problem of urban poverty is, all other things being equal, it is more serious the darker one's skin is. The report of the Kerner Commission, set up by President Johnson, and several studies by the U.S. Department of Labor [14] have described the following important characteristics of urban black poverty and employment during the 1966–70 period:

1. Black people had jobs at the lower end of the income and status scale: while about 40 percent of the urban white labor force was employed in professional, clerical, or managerial jobs, only 15 to 20 percent of black employees held such jobs; and while one-tenth of the white labor force worked in low-skilled service or laboring jobs, over *one-third* of the blacks did.

2. Blacks make less income than whites at *every* educational level. Though this discrepancy may in part stem from inferior education and training (which itself is due largely to racism in the past) recent data indicate that this factor is a quite significant measure of *current* discriminatory practices.

14. Especially Robert Kitgaard, "The Dual Labor Market and Manpower Policy," *Monthly Labor Review*, November, 1971, pp. 45–48.

3. The incidence of poverty, as defined by the Federal government, was about two to three times greater among black families than among white ones in American urban areas in 1968. This amounted to about 25–30 percent of all black families.

4. Poverty was more than twice as prevalent among nonwhite families with female heads than among those with male heads in 1966. In central cities, 26 percent of all nonwhite families of two or more persons had female heads, as compared to 12 percent of white families. *Eighty-one* percent of the female-headed families with children under six—about *240,000 families in central cities* —were classified as poor by the Federal government.

6. The unemployment rate among urban blacks is usually about twice that of whites for the nation as a whole, and about three times as high for blacks in slum areas; among black teenagers, the unemployment rate has hovered around 25–35 percent during 1965–1970.

7. The "subemployment" index (including, in general, the unemployed, *plus* the only sporadically employed and those working full-time at less than the poverty income) is always much higher for blacks than for any other group. In ghetto economies the rate has been about *one-third* of the black labor force during the past few years. Many observers feel that the subemployment index rate is a better indication of the relationship of blacks to labor markets than the usual unemployment rate.

Of course, these figures seriously underestimate the dimensions of urban black poverty and unemployment, even when given in relative terms, because they still concentrate on income and employment figures. There are many other features of being black and poor which subtract from a black family's low income in addition to the several—unequal treatment before the law, poor education opportunities and health care—which were mentioned earlier as factors that significantly lowered the real income of *all* the urban poor.

Take, for example, expenditures on housing. The amount of housing available to an urban black family is less than that available to a white family, all other socioeconomic characteristics of the two families being similar. This fact has never been seriously doubted by any but the most obtuse observers. The effect of this, of course, is that prices paid for scarce housing by blacks include an additional payment, a subtraction from the real incomes of blacks when compared with white incomes. If blacks pay a premium for housing, then their real income is lower, by some amount, then the real income of a white person with a similar money income. Additionally, John Kain has shown that since buying houses since World War II has been an especially good source of accumulating wealth and capital gains, the *real* cost to blacks of housing-market discrimination has been greater even than that implied in simple models of housing discrimination. In an article written with John Quigley, Kain has suggested that the total effect of such discrimination, "under some reasonable assumptions," could have amounted to a monthly markup in housing of as much as 50 percent for urban blacks in the period since 1949.[15] This housing-market discrimination exists at all levels of the urban housing industry. Thus, the choice of housing, even among the very poorest of the poor, is a more costly choice for a black family than for a white one, and the premium is paid whether the housing purchased is rented or owned.

A second example of the relative disadvantage of being black, as well as poor, is that black neighborhoods with an average family income of, say, four thousand dollars may typically be less satisfying to their residents than a similar white neighborhood. There are several possible explanations for this tendency. First, white neighborhoods generally get better public services than black neighborhoods because of the greater sympathy afforded them by white local governments. There can be little doubt about this matter, and for proof most of us need only drive across town. Second, the threshold of opportunity in each neighborhood is probably quite different, in the sense that for the white family with a four thousand dollar income there exists a greater possibility for upward mobility and a greater range of choice in housing and employment decisions. The black neigh-

15. John Kain and John Quigley, "Housing Market Discrimination, Homeownership and Savings Behavior," Program on Regional and Urban Economics, Discussion Paper no. 58 (Cambridge: Harvard University Press, 1970).

borhood will include more families who *want* to move out but can't; this conclusion follows logically from any theory of involuntary segregation. Finally, the white neighborhood will be less likely to be a reception center for waves of lower-income migrants, who compound the problems of whatever particular neighborhood to which they migrate.

These two examples of why the black poor have lower real income than the white poor with identical money incomes could be extended, and most of the additional examples would be obvious ones. The point is quite simply that the dimensions of black poverty are *especially* prone to underestimation by government poverty statistics. Thus, data indicating that one-third of all urban blacks are poor probably underestimate the problem considerably. In all likelihood, more than half are provided with inadequate goods and services, and an even greater proportion are denied the full range of choices taken for granted by whites. To be black in America is to pay, out of whatever level of income you make, some monetary premium for American racism; unfortunately, no one knows *what* that premium is.

III. Theories of Urban Black Poverty

More difficult than trying to count the urban black poor, though this has been judged close to impossible, is trying to adequately explain their poverty. The previous chapter identified several different theories of poverty, theories which typically pay special attention to black poverty. If one surveyed all the different theories of black poverty, one would find two major kinds. The first would be similar to the works of academics like Banfield, Kain, and Thurow, whose studies tend to explain black poverty in terms of the special characteristics of most urban blacks: their age, sex, job-training experience, proximity to urban labor markets, etc.[16] These theories imply that the main problem with poor blacks is their special characteristics: to change their

16. In the following chapter, I will show how the graduate training of most economists prepares them to do Thurow-Kain–type model building, but not to handle some of the clearest implications of their own work.

income level, one must change these special characteristics. What is important here is the clear implication of this kind of model that poverty can be eliminated when the special characteristics of poor blacks are changed.

The second kind of theory emerging from a survey of black poverty is embodied in models—such as those discussed in Chapter 1—which explain it as a fault of the industrial capitalist system, an obvious implication being that such poverty has less to do with the personal characteristics of black people than with the need of such a system for an underclass. Not surprisingly, therefore, the first kind of theorists, those who think poverty can be solved within the system, are concerned with changing *absolute* income levels, and it is this measure of income which they tend to emphasize. The more radical theorists tend, almost always, to emphasize relative poverty, and to suggest that the triumph of liberal reform would leave a great residue of poverty; there would still be the upper class, the middle class, and the lower class, with the whole hierarchy simply at a higher level of income. I will discuss in the following two chapters the implications for social policy which flow from these two types of model building, but I have digressed here a moment to emphasize what has been hinted at throughout this and the previous discussion: *the way one conceptualizes the problem of poverty is the single most important determinant of the kind of policy one finally contrives as the best solution to poverty.* The importance of this fairly obvious assertion cannot be overestimated.

IV. The Liberal Theory of Black Poverty

In any case, let's take a look at the two kinds of models. I shall start with the "special characteristics" models of Kain, Banfield, and others, and, for lack of better terminology, shall refer to them as "liberal academic" explanations of black poverty. I am using the term "liberal" to identify those academic writers who share the view that it is possible to solve the problem of poverty within an industrial capitalist system. The second group shall be referred to as "radical theorists," again for lack of better terminology, and consists of those who are convinced that capitalism breeds poverty and that the poor are thus as inevitable a consequence of such a system as are the rich.

The academic liberal view in these matters does not seriously conflict with the historical survey offered earlier. In general, liberals agree that blacks who came in great numbers to the cities were poor, unskilled, and hopeful, and that most were disappointed when they got there. Their disappointment derived primarily from certain characteristics of the urban labor market and the urban economy for which they had not been prepared. Especially surprising to them was that during the same time they were migrating from the South, whites were taking an increasing amount of work to the suburbs, to some extent precisely because the blacks had arrived in the central city. Most firms, however, probably left the city for more concrete economic or aesthetic reasons: tax rates, rent, access to new highways, access to suburban workers, or simply an urge to leave the decaying central city. Naturally, given these changes in the overall spatial characteristics of the metropolitan area, the typical black residential area was increasingly characterized by high unemployment rates and extensive poverty. And as the number of migrants increased, much, much, faster than the core economy could absorb them, the unemployment and poverty rates grew higher and higher. Indeed, the black section of town, by the fifties, and almost always in the sixties, became more frequently referred to as the "ghetto," signifying its increasing size and segregation from the rest of the city. Since the number of poor had increased, intensifying all the problems blacks had always had in the central city, their problems increased, and in the public mind they became "crises."

Interestingly, the Federal government played a very large role in events which led to the crisis of black poverty in large metropolitan ghettos. I will briefly review that argument, for it is closely related to the liberal theory of black poverty and its implications for public policy. The major share of Federal spending in urban areas between 1955 and 1970 was allocated to two programs. The first, the urban highway program, which will eventually lead to about seven thousand miles of urban highways financed largely by the Federal government, provided quick exit and entry to the central city and made it possible to live in the suburbs and do business in town without serious inconvenience.[17] Families with adequate incomes could seek housing space in the suburbs, away from the madding crowd downtown. And they did. Of course, one important reason they could was that since 1935 the FHA program had subsidized the purchase of suburban houses for over seven million *non*poor families.[18] In 1966, for example, 99 *percent* of the recipients of FHA-insured loans had incomes over four thousand dollars, and the overwhelming majority of these families, and others in the long history of the program, were white.

In addition, because of the inflation in land costs, building costs, and interest rates, in 1970 there were *no* houses subsidized by the FHA which cost *less* than ten thousand dollars. This policy, of course, excludes over half the public—black, brown, or white—from buying houses under the program. Finally, the FHA had encouraged segregation in a more direct way by refusing most loans to all but white suburban homeowners. William Tabb, in his excellent book *The Political Economy of the Black Ghetto,* has summarized this policy as follows:

> The FHA . . . for many years took the position that racial homogeneity was essential to a neighborhood's financial stability. It therefore placed higher valuations on properties in neighborhoods that were white than . . . mixed. This policy served as a powerful inducement to segregation. After restrictive racial covenants in deeds were held . . . unconstitutional [in 1948], the FHA stopped insuring properties where such covenants applied. But it continued to tolerate discrimination, providing insurance where builders would not sell, mortgagors would not lend, and owners would not rent to Negroes. In 1962 . . . an executive order . . . forbade discrimination in the sale or rental of all

17. For an informative muckraking account of the role of government and industry in the development of the interstate highway system, see Helen Leavitt, *Superhighway: Superhoax* (Garden City: Doubleday, 1970).

18. Almost all the relevant facts and figures on Federal housing policies are in National Commission on Urban Problems, *Building the American City* (New York: Praeger, 1969). Some of the data here are from various Federal census publications.

housing owned or financed by government. But it applied
only to future transactions. . . . At the same time that the
FHA was encouraging segregation, it was redistributing real
income from general taxation to the non-poor homeowners. Until August 1967, the FHA, by denying mortgage insurance programs to buyers in blighted areas . . . did not help blacks become homeowners in their own restricted housing markets. . . .[19]

Thus, the Federal government paid a major part of the bill for
decentralizing the city after 1955. It paid for the highways to
get to the suburbs, and helped pay for the homes that mostly
only middle-class (or wealthier) whites could buy in the suburbs. Moreover, because of tax considerations, the changing
technology of manufacturing, and other factors, business firms
also began to migrate, taking with them most of the good jobs,
especially those manufacturing jobs which pay good wages for
relatively unskilled work. Of course, while spending its funds for
highway building and housing subsidies, the Federal government consistently avoided using its own revenue to supplement
the increasingly strained budgets of many large central cities. As
a consequence of this deteriorating fiscal situation, a rapidly
growing problem for large cities in the 1960's, the supply of metropolitan services began to fall behind the need for them. Thus,
the employment problems of new migrants to the large cities
were compounded by a speedy deterioration in the quantity and
quality of public services, especially in poor areas.

THE CULTURE OF POVERTY

Two dimensions of black ghettos which developed as a result of
government policy and for other reasons have received special
attention by liberal theorists, and are integral parts of the liberal analysis of black poverty. The first of these involves a clus-
ter of behavioral patterns called the "culture of poverty." [20] This

19. New York: Norton, 1970, pp. 16–17. See also Theodore F. Lowi, *The
End of Liberalism* (Norton, 1969), Chapter 9.
20. Lewis's work has been cited earlier. For a recent collection of views
on the matter, see Eleanor Burke Leacock, ed., *The Culture of Poverty: A
Critique* (New York: Simon and Schuster, 1971).

image, first suggested by Oscar Lewis, and borrowed by a great number of urbanologists (including, by the way, Banfield), attempts to provide an analytical framework in which to study the sociological, economic, and psychological characteristics which so frequently describe the urban poor (especially the poor in an industrialized, capitalist society). The "culture of poverty" argument goes something like this: a poor ghetto—whether black, Puerto Rican, Irish, or WASP—has its own particular ethos, a considerable range of behavioral characteristics displayed by its members which makes their plight insensitive to most antipoverty measures, including income flows. John Kenneth Galbraith's "insular and case poverty" (in *The Affluent Society*),[21] and Banfield's "lower-class behavior" are both attempts to symbolize those kinds of personal characteristics which make the poor "different" from other Americans. Such traits as helplessness, despair, a relatively strong propensity to break laws written by others, large numbers of illegitimate children, family size considerably beyond the capacity of family income, a tendency to be impulsive and present-oriented, fatherless families, and, especially important, a harsh and defeating self-contempt—all are said to lead to a life style outside the mainstream of American economic and social life.

In this kind of analysis it is assumed that most of the black poor have been conditioned to think of themselves as unworthy or unable to compete in labor markets, and that ultimately there is established a vicious circle of behavior in which the belief in one's inability to compete in labor markets leads to a life style inconsistent with competition. In addition, since the better-paying jobs are no longer accessible to many central-city dwellers, even when the poor work their jobs are typically low-paying and/or demeaning. The job therefore becomes further evidence of their unworthiness in their own eyes and in everyone else's. Therefore, as an alleged consequence of this "subculture," flourishing in most poverty areas is the "irregular economy:" prostitutes, hustlers, numbers runners, petty and major criminals, increasing numbers of welfare recipients, and other human beings

21. Chapter xxiii.

who evidence the breakdown in the effectiveness of the regular economy.

The "culture of poverty" argument has appeared especially relevant in explaining the "cycle of poverty." To be raised in a poor family is to acquire, at a *very early* age, all those characteristics which will ultimately lead to a life of poverty. Poor education, an inadequate diet, low-quality health care, bickering and frustration among the parents, a life on the streets—all are assumed to be sufficient ingredients to assure that a poor person's children will also be poor. The "culture of poverty" theory has become, in most liberal circles, a theory of the social conditions of slums, by which the personal characteristics of the poor leading to their low incomes are a result of their having lived in a poor neighborhood. One simply does not acquire the habits of being punctual, competitive, neat, orderly, or upwardly mobile if one has been raised in a ghetto neighborhood. The reader is probably familiar with this kind of argument if he or she has read anything about urban poverty written during the past decade.

Of course, the "culture of poverty" thesis immediately provoked numerous critics, especially because of the assumption implicit in the analysis that poor people were somehow "different" from the rest of us.[22] Additionally, as many writers pointed out, the Lewis argument carried with it a rather crucial political implication (which we discussed at some length in Chapter 1): the poverty of the poor was the result of their own peculiar characteristics, rather than being a necessary consequence of an industrial order—such as a capitalist one—which depends upon the existence of an underclass. Charles Valentine, an urban anthropologist, has stated succinctly this political implication of the "culture of poverty" argument by suggesting that it

> . . . enables Americans to evade hard questions about changes in the distribution of resources and the structure of society needed to resolve the problem of inequality which is the essence of the poverty crisis. It is used not only to silence radical critiques of our social system but also to calm the doubts of liberals

22. See especially Leacock's Introduction and Bibliography.

or others that the system may not be working as it is supposed to. Faith in the status quo can be kept intact with no more than minor adjustment in national priorities. At the same time, slogans like 'culture of poverty' confer a gratifying feeling that a fresh understanding of a lingering difficulty has been achieved. The policy lines and action programs which flow from this may, for a time at least, create a comforting sense of new and promising practical initiatives.[23]

My purpose here is not to discuss this debate about the relative merits of the "culture of poverty" argument, though I happen to agree with Valentine's essential point. What is more important, at least in the present context, is that, *right or wrong,* the "culture of poverty" argument largely determined the principal features of the liberal antipoverty efforts of the 1960's. Indeed, some of the severest criticism of the argument has resulted precisely because the critics believed social policy was being based on incorrect social theory.

RACISM IN LIBERAL MODELS OF POVERTY

A second dimension of the liberal theory of poverty which has played a crucial role in the theory's development is the varying emphasis which liberals place on "racism" as a causative determinant of black poverty. All liberal theorists are aware that discrimination, or racism, plays a role in black poverty, and even Banfield, though he tries to deemphasize this dimension of the problem, admits that it exists. Racism is usually seen in these models as a barrier to the black poor which exists for them along with all of those suffered by the white poor. John Kain, for example, has done a great deal of work trying to show that racial discrimination in housing and in urban labor markets significantly decreases the possibility for black workers to get an adequate income, even for those who are willing and able to do work in better jobs.[24] He has presented considerable data show-

23. Charles Valentine, "The Culture of Poverty: Its Scientific Significance and Its Implication for Action," in Leacock, p. 216.
24. See the following articles by John Kain, as representative of his work in this general area: "Theories of Residential Location and Realities of Race," Harvard Program on Regional and Urban Economics, Discussion

ing that at the same time the better-paying jobs were moving to the suburbs, there were arising significant barriers between black workers and those jobs. First, there were the barriers in the housing and labor markets which we referred to earlier. Second, there were barriers in the transportation system because Federal money had gone into the construction of urban highways, giving access mainly to those who had cars. Since ownership of autos is the special province of those with adequate income to buy them, and since the metropolitan public transportation system began dying simultaneously with the growth of urban highways, the inner-city poor were cut off from access to jobs in the suburbs.

Lester Thurow, another econometrician whose work was mentioned earlier, ended his most important study of black poverty by arguing that programs to lessen black poverty will not succeed unless something is done to end discrimination.[25] Though the injection of racial discrimination into the liberal model of poverty seriously complicates that kind of analysis, its general conclusions survive the complication quite nicely. If you read the liberal theorist carefully, it is clear that this awareness of racial discrimination has not led to a change in the basic features of liberal models, which still seek to explain poverty as the result of the personal characteristics of the poor. In these revised models of poverty there is for the black person, quite simply, a new personal characteristic to be considered.

In general, emerging from the liberal theory of poverty is a "war" on poverty consisting of three kinds of programs: the first kind is aimed at destroying the culture of poverty (through programs such as the Model Cities Program, Community Action Agencies, and urban renewal); the second kind of program tries

Paper no. 47 (Cambridge: Harvard University Press, 1969); an article with John Meyer, "The Interrelationship Between Transportation and Poverty," *The Public Interest*, Winter, 1970; "The Distribution and Movement of Jobs and Industry," in James Wilson, ed., *The Metropolitan Enigma* (Garden City: Doubleday, 1970); "Postwar Metropolitan Development, Housing Preference and Auto Ownership," *American Economic Review*, May, 1967; and "Housing Segregation, Negro Employment and Metropolitan Decentralization," *Quarterly Journal of Economics*, May, 1968.

25. *Poverty and Discrimination* (Washington, D.C.: Brookings Institution, 1969).

to change the personal characteristics of the poor (day care, Head Start, job training, the Job Corps, special education funds for low-income neighborhoods, school-busing); and, finally, there are programs in liberal policy aimed at reducing discrimination in urban markets (such as the Philadelphia Plan, under which the Federal government attempts to force private contractors to train and hire minority groups to work on government construction projects; the recent Department of Housing and Urban Development denial of funds for housing programs which increase residential segregation; and civil rights legislation).[26] These kinds of programs follow quite logically from the liberal theory of poverty and its implied assumption that absolute poverty can be ended, or at least minimized, by changing the personal characteristics of the poor—by changing either their abilities or the *immediate* environments in which they live, work, or go to school.

What it is absolutely essential to realize about this kind of theory and the policies that derive from it is that they are based upon the assumption that it is possible to end absolute poverty in an industrial capitalist society. Not surprisingly, this basic assumption is rejected by a few theorists, mostly on the left; their models are discussed below.

V. Radical Theories of Urban Black Poverty

Consider a quotation from two Marxists, Paul Baran and Paul Sweezy. In their discussion of racism in American society, they invoke images that are distinctly different from those of the liberals concerning the reasons for black poverty:

> [In a monopoly capitalist society] it thus happens that a special pariah group [pariah from the point of view of those above] at the bottom acts as a kind of lightning rod for the frustrations and hostilities of all the higher groups, the more so the nearer they are to the bottom. It may even be said that the very existence of the pariah group is a kind of harmonizer and stabilizer

26. I shall spend some time in Chapter 4 further discussing these programs.

of the social structure—so long as the pariahs play their role passively. Such a society becomes in time so thoroughly saturated with race prejudice that it sinks below the level of consciousness and becomes a part of the "human nature" of it members. . . . Status being a relative matter, whites inevitably interpret upward movement by Negroes as downward movement for themselves. This complex of attitudes . . . provides an important part of the explanation why whites not only refuse to help Negroes rise, but bitterly resist their efforts to do so. . . .[27]

There are several elements in this statement that distinguishes its tone from that of liberal theories. Notice first that it is assumed by Baran and Sweezy that the existence of a lower class is a *necessary and inevitable consequence* of a mature industrial capitalist system. Of course, such a statement is quite consistent with the observed historical tendency in all market economies for there to be considerable wealth at one end of the income distribution scale and considerable deprivation at the other. The point is, however, that from this particular Marxist point of view, the liberal theory is based upon a rather strange belief that somehow it is possible to eliminate the underclass even though this has never occurred in a capitalist society. During the present generation, it is the blacks who are the poor urban underclass; once it was the Italians, before them the Irish, before them someone else, and before them someone else. Since elimination of the underclass in capitalism has never happened before, why spend time explaining how to achieve the impossible?

A second implication of the Baran and Sweezy statement follows from the assumption of the inevitability of the lower class and concerns the function this class serves for the rest of society. Their argument, explicit and implied, is that the competitive social order feeds upon the existence of losers. The competitive personality is stymied by games in which nobody loses; think of how few of us can actually enjoy games without a winner, or of the wage-earner whose first ten thousand dollars only sets the stage for the second, or of the professor whose concern for the

27. *Monopoly Capital* (New York: Monthly Review Press, 1966), pp. 265–266.

truth is overwhelmed by his need to *know more than anyone else* about a particular subject, and, especially, consider the capitalist whose first million is but the basis for making more millions. It is absolutely necessary in such a social order to have losers, lest the value of winning lose some of its special appeal. And, further, in such a social order, efforts to abolish the lower class and its deprivation—in this case disproportionately the problem of urban blacks—are impeded at a subconscious level by the needs of the upper classes to be reminded continually of their relative success in the competitive social order. Though consciously aware of the poverty problem, we institute antipoverty programs which are underfinanced, based on inadequate or inaccurate social theory, halfheartedly carried out, and drained unmercifully by local bureaucracies, because at the base of our collective psyche is the awesome fear that abolishing the lower class will also abolish a considerable source of our own self-esteem.

Consider, finally, a third implication of the statement by Baran and Sweezy. According to these Marxists, market discrimination is not just an important cause of the relative disadvantage of blacks, but an important outward manifestation of a "thoroughly saturated" racist social order. Such a definition of racism does not imply the kind which is subject to change by Federal laws, school-busing, and civil rights legislation. It implies an attitude on the part of whites and a resultant attitude on the part of blacks which have become strong elements of the "human nature" of each race. A competitive order intensifies the kinds of racist tendencies which people seem to have had throughout human history. In other words, in the view of these Marxists, and most other radicals, black poverty reflects racism (and liberal theorists would, of course, agree with this idea), but, to the radical, racism is a function, to a *very* important degree, of the nature of the *system;* capitalism, because it is competitive and aggressive, exacerbates whatever racial or other prejudices one may have to begin with.

The point here is that Baran and Sweezy identify a different kind of model, an alternative approach to explaining the poverty of black urban Americans. They suggest that the capitalist order, as it has developed over time, has made it necessary to have an underclass, and that the latest underclass, because of migration patterns, because of the pattern of American history, because of a host of other variables, has disproportionately become black and urban.

Let me briefly reinterpret the data on black poverty from this radical perspective.[28] We have identified the major variables in the liberal theory as black migration, suburbanization of white business and white residents, the role of the Federal government in urban highway-building and subsidization of white residential suburban home-building, and the racial attitudes of white Americans. We have described the result of all this, which nobody seriously disagrees with, as black central cities with a high incidence of poverty, and great islands where the "culture of poverty" tends to overwhelm everything else.

A radical analysis of these variables would explain the black migration which started it all as having roots in the southern agricultural economy of the nineteenth century. In this economy, radicals have argued, white plantation-owners used the slavery of blacks—begun by capitalist traders in the seventeenth and eighteenth centuries—as a basis for temporary domination of the nation's cotton industry; by keeping slaves in bondage, white southerners were able to establish an essentially feudal social order, ended only by their unsuccessful war with the North. By the *late* nineteenth century, though freed from literal slavery in the South, American blacks became the victims of "Jim Crow," which replaced the slave institutions of earlier times with a new kind of racism, less frequently sanctified by law, but real nonetheless. This institutional racism, which con-

28. The radical literature on urban blacks and their problems is already voluminous and is growing at a faster rate, unfortunately, than any single human can keep up with. I have included in the Bibliography a section on the subject which contains many such analyses. Also, for current information, one should stay abreast of the following periodicals, which ordinarily include, among others, articles by writers who take a radical stance on this issue: *Monthly Review, Social Policy, Review of Black Political Economy, Review of Radical Political Economy, Socialist Revolution, Black Scholar,* and *Dissent.* There are, of course, many other periodicals which present the radical view, but those mentioned here are among the most accessible and certainly among the most informative.

tinues very powerfully to haunt this country, has had many effects on American blacks, not the least of which has been their gradual restriction to two kinds of labor: low-paying jobs in cities and low-paying agricultural labor in rural areas.

Thus, as almost everyone knows by now, today's urban black poverty did not start with the failure of agricultural labor to compete with machines: it started when slave-traders tore Africans from their homeland like any cargo that could profitably be sold. Today's racism, therefore, which is found in a hundred million interstices of the social fabric of this country, had its origins in the steerage of a thousand ships which sailed the sea over two centuries ago.

Given this historical foundation to the radical theory, almost everything else in the model follows logically. Blacks have been kept at the bottom of the social order since their first step onto this land; thus, they are the latest immigrants to the city, having been kept in the South first as slaves for cotton-based southern feudalism, then as marginal tenant farmers and domestic service workers after Reconstruction. They live in central cities today, with no access to the suburbs, first because they are relatively unskilled, second because they are black.

In addition to concentrating on the historical origins of today's urban black poverty, the radical would also emphasize the state's role in the current features of the problem. It has already been mentioned that to the liberal academic, the state's role in the matter is as the Grand Reformer: witness the wars on poverty, income-maintenance programs, and all the other Federal antipoverty programs. To the radical, dependence on the state for reform is the weakest part of the liberal imagination. The radical would hypothesize as a logical result of his theory of the state that it reflects the needs of those who own it, the capitalist class.[29] To prove this, the radical would reinterpret the role of the state in creating the latest affliction of American urban blacks. Was it not the state which built the urban highways so that the white middle class could move from the core and take a significant part of the central city economy and tax base with it?

29. A concise statement of the radical theory of the state is in Paul Sweezy, *The Theory of Capitalist Development* (New York: Oxford University Press, 1942), Chapter 13.

Was it not the state which financed suburban home-building for the middle and upper class? And was it not the liberal-reform New Deal Federal government in the 1930's which began the construction of public housing in the central cities, which. among other things, effectively sealed low-income people into the central cities? And, to top it all off, hasn't Richard Nixon appealed to southern racism, and racism in American suburbs, in his campaigns for the presidency?

In general, the radical proceeds to investigate all the various parts of the social order which seem to have a bearing on the problem at hand: the historical context, the political order, various theories of psychology, sociology, and, finally, economics. The principal difference between this kind of analysis and that of the liberal is that a large part of the latter concentrates on the personal characteristics of the poor, and thus turns out to be an analysis of the very tip of an enormous iceberg. The underside of the iceberg is hidden by an incredibly complex social order, an organism with a past history and a current life of its own, whose larger secrets are utterly hidden from those who concentrate on only one aspect of it. Not surprisingly, the political conclusions deriving from such differing methodologies are themselves quite different.

This discussion of urban black poverty, especially the review of the differing theories of poverty, leads us to two important questions. The first question, which has been hinted at throughout the earlier discussion, regards the political response implied by the different models of poverty we have been discussing. Such responses are the subject of the final two chapters of this book. A second question which emerges from this discussion concerns the two types of theories discussed, liberal and radical. I have intentionally not taken up in detail the explanation of *why* some economists are liberal and others are radical; this is the subject of the next chapter. In essence, Chapter 3 seeks to demonstrate that the prescriptions for public policy which come from the experts are *inherent* in the way they study the problem they seek to solve. "Show me your model and I'll tell you your politics": to the defense of this outlandish claim I now turn.

Chapter Three

ECONOMICS AND BLACK POVERTY

The Methodology of Contemporary Liberal Economics

Most academic economists are liberal in the sense that term is being used here. Radical economists, on the other hand, though a growing lot, are still in a very distinct minority and continue to be considered, with varying degrees of condescension, a fringe element on the scene. The most famous American economists—Paul Samuelson, John K. Galbraith, Arthur Burns, Paul McCracken, to name only a few—are all apparently committed to the view that poverty can be eliminated within the basic institutions of an advanced capitalist order. And when their optimism is challenged by the persistent mass poverty throughout American history, liberals ordinarily respond by presenting data (like those in Chapter 1) showing that "the number of poor has decreased significantly especially since 1960."

What lies behind the liberal's faith in the system, in his or her undying allegiance to the basic features of a social order which is so obviously destructive of many of its least prepared members? What follows is an attempt to illuminate this issue by linking economic liberalism firmly to the methodological approach economists are trained to use. Though methodological background is not the only determinant of the typical economist's liberalism, it is a crucial enough variable to be given special consideration.

I. The Liberal Economist and America's Social Problems

Until quite recently, economists dealt with black poverty mainly by ignoring it. This should not, however, be interpreted as indicating any specific bias on their part. Indeed, economists also largely ignored—and many still do—the population problem, environmental pollution, the increasing involvement of the military in industry and government, the collapse of metropolitan services, urban congestion, the degeneration of public education, and, generally, the rapid decline in the quality of life in America.

Probably the main cause of this gross neglect of so many very important things was the typical economist's profound belief—a belief that many still maintain—that most problems in this nation could be solved, or at least relieved, by full employment and by a growth in the national economy. The fascination with and dependence upon economic growth is readily understandable in terms of the dramatic change that occurred in economic thought during the 1930's. The thirties were a dreadful experience for many Americans, and according to most accounts, the scene was equally dismal for most industrial nations in the Western world. The collapse of the stock market in this country in 1929 ushered in a decade of depression, a depression which was terminated only by massive war expenditures in the 1940's.

Orthodox economists had spent no little energy between 1815 and 1930 demonstrating that, contrary to Marxian and other warnings, depression and the attendant mass unemployment were impossible. Therefore, they were understandably, if not pitifully, reluctant to admit to the limitation of their theories in explaining what went wrong.[1] No doubt this firm support of a losing theoretical cause was encouraged by such stands as that taken by a famous nineteenth-century economist, David Ricardo. When confronted with observed facts which contradicted his theoretical conclusions, he is said to have replied: "So much the worse for the facts." Such was the unhappy position of many American economists in the early 1930's.

The reputation of professional economists—at a low in the mid-thirties which is approached only by their current disrepute [2]—was salvaged in 1936, ironically, by an unorthodox but brilliant economic theorist, John Maynard Keynes.[3] Keynes reoriented the thinking of an entire generation of Western economists by producing a theoretical framework which dictated a radically different role for the central government than that advocated by the nineteenth-century classical tradition. In essence, Keynes suggested what was apparent to those who had not been inflicted with faith in pre-Keynesian economic theory: there were no inherent reasons why the economy should reach equilibrium at full employment, and in a recession the government should cut taxes, increase spending, or both. The tax cut of 1964 and the surtax of 1968 are both examples of the effect of the Keynesian revolution on policy makers. (Interestingly, the wage-price freeze of 1971 has added to the rather dismal record of many macroeconomists, who argued, along with Keynes, that

1. In describing the general level of pre-Keynesian theories of depression, Edmund Whittaker wrote in 1940 that "if reputable economists neglected [the subject of depression] it was only expected that others would fill the gap—just as quack doctors at county fairs do a thriving trade in mysterious remedies' for the common complaints for which professional men have no cure" (A History of Economic Ideas [New York: Longmans, Green, 1940], p. 713).

2. For a similar argument, see Edwin Dale, Jr., "The Unfavourables," New York Times, November 7, 1971, p. 7f.

3. In his classic treatise The Theory of Income, Employment and Money (New York: Harcourt, Brace, 1936).

in order to reduce inflation—which has plagued the U.S. especially since 1965—it is necessary to slow down the rate of growth in total output [GNP]. When the price level failed to respond to restrictive tax and spending policies, the Nixon Administration reacted with Phases I and II, both aimed at stabilizing the price level without at the same time slowing down GNP and increasing unemployment. To put the best face on all these attempts at social engineering, they didn't work.[4])

What is important, for our purposes, is that the Keynesian system made it possible to end, temporarily anyway, the supreme agony in the history of capitalist economies, the unpredictable business cycle. These periodic depressions were for the working class a personal disaster, and for the ruling class a threat to stability and thus a threat to their own power. To most orthodox economists, unemployment and the resulting mass insecurity had always been the worst features of a capitalist system and the most difficult to understand. Thus, the promise of Keynesian fiscal and monetary policy as a way of moderating the business cycle and making it more predictable were rightly hailed as a major breakthrough. So it was with economists by, say, 1945. The Keynesian revolution, in fact, became politicized in the United States in 1946 when the Employment Act created the Council of Economic Advisors. To this day the CEA is staffed, for the most part, by Keynesian economists. And even though there is rather impressive evidence that President Eisenhower never understood the new theory, all other presidents since 1946 have accepted it as an established feature of their strategies.

What should be emphasized here is that economists in the 1950's accepted the idea that the problem of sustained production had been solved—theoretically, if not politically—and this implied clearly that if there were poor people, their problem would be solved by increasing output. If full-employment output grew enough, the argument went, eventually labor markets would grow so tight that everyone—the unskilled, uneducated, unkempt, and even uncivilized—would finally be absorbed into

4. Compare my generalizations with evaluations of macroeconomic forecasting which have appeared in the business press during the past eighteen months (since about the early part of 1971).

gainful employment. Thus, given this faith in full-employment GNP as a *necessary* prerequisite to solving most human problems, it is not surprising that by 1960, with a few notable exceptions, American economists had not concerned themselves very much with the problem of poverty—black, white, red, or any other kind.

The relative neglect of poverty by economists prior to the 1960's was also, to some extent, due to the fact that poverty was not a political issue of great note during these years. Economists, like most other students of society, tend to concentrate on what seem the most pressing problems—with some time lags, of course—and the principal political issues immediately following the Keynesian revolution in the 1930's were war and cold war, which demanded concentration on the size of GNP rather than on its distribution. Thus, the continuing faith in GNP today as a way to solve our most pressing problems is probably an understandable carryover from the 1940–60 period. At any rate, during the 1950's, two separate features of the American economy not sufficiently dealt with in the simple Keynesian model emerged to upset the tenuous equilibrium which existed between the economists and their subject matter. The first, inflation and unemployment occurring simultaneously, will be discussed later. The second feature was the persistence of unemployment and poverty in certain subcultures of the society. The most famous of the several discussions of this phenomenon written by an economist is Galbraith's *The Affluent Society*.[5] In his book, Galbraith argued that the expansion of the economy increased the income of everyone except those trapped in what he called "insular" and "case" poverty. Thus, uneducated rural whites, the aged, the sick, and the racial minorities were included in a large, varied group whose unifying characteristic was that some were unlikely to benefit at all from a growing national economy.

Galbraith argued persuasively that we needed to shift the emphasis of our inquiry from the aggregate economy into its separate parts to understand poverty. In the jargon of theoretical

5. Boston: Houghton-Mifflin, 1958.

economics, this meant shifting from an emphasis on macroeconomics to the microeconomics of poverty subcultures. This shift in emphasis also helped to divide most economists into two separate schools about how to solve poverty: the "expansionists" maintained faith that a growing GNP would finally absorb the poor into gainful employment; the "structuralists," such as Charles Killingsworth,[6] expanded on the Galbraithian theme. More about these camps later.

The initial clamor made by Galbraith in 1958, however, was completely overshadowed by the publication in 1962 of Michael Harrington's *The Other America*,[7] a more detailed description of poverty by a radical Catholic socialist. According to legend, the most important feature of this book, aside from the passion of its message and its assertion that forty to fifty million Americans were poor, was that John Kennedy discovered poverty when he read it. His reading of the book, to continue the legend, initiated a series of government programs which culminated after his death in the so-called War on Poverty (discussed in Chapter 4). Thus, in the early and mid-sixties, poverty was made public and politicized, and increasingly during the decade, especially after the urban riots, the issue of black poverty began to emerge as one of the most important aspects of the performance of the American economy.

In general, in addition to a lot of head counting, economists have reacted to black poverty by doing two kinds of related theoretical work. Some economists, like Gary Becker of Columbia, have developed models based on microeconomics and mathematics to determine the monetary costs of discrimination, assuming different market structures. One major limitation of Becker's study [8] is that, like many microtheorists, he assumes that participants in his theoretical world are motivated solely by

6. Charles Killingsworth, "Automation, Jobs and Manpower" (statement before 1963 Senate Subcommittee on Employment and Manpower), reprinted in *Labor and the National Economy*, ed. William G. Bowen (New York: Norton, 1965). This article exemplifies Killingsworth's work in the area.

7. New York: Macmillan, 1962.

8. Gary Becker, *The Economics of Discrimination* (Chicago: University of Chicago Press, 1957).

economic considerations, unconstrained by non-economic variables; this assumption makes the resulting analysis both stilted and unconvincing.

Another major question raised by many critics of this kind of work—few of them economists—is whether it is even possible to quantify *all* the costs of discrimination, or even its more harmful ones. That is, the statistical measurement of only those costs of discrimination which can be expressed in money terms and can be counted may result only in the misleading notion that the other, nonmeasurable, effects of discrimination are somehow less important than the measurable ones. The total costs of discrimination against blacks, in addition to the money costs which can be measured, may include, among others: ignominy, self-doubt and even self-hatred, humiliation, fear, hunger, deprivation, etc., etc. Thus, the economist who would try to measure these effects by assigning them a money cost, or who would ignore them because they cannot be analyzed systematically, only fools himself or herself.[9]

A second type of theoretical and empirical work on black poverty has been done by econometricians, and their work is different only to a small degree from the type of work done by Becker. The major distinction between these two kinds of analyses is that econometricians try to derive empirically the basic features of their model, though, like Becker, they generally assume that the human participants in their models are motivated solely by the desire for economic gain. The work of one eminent econometrician, Lester Thurow, was discussed in the previous chapter. I should like to be a bit more explicit here about econometricians and their work, especially as it relates to social policy.

An econometrician's reasoning is roughly as follows: It is assumed that black poverty exists and that its principal characteristics and causes can be measured statistically.[10] *Question:* What is black poverty related to that can be measured?

9. See note 30, Chapter 1.
10. A fairly clear presentation of econometric fundamentals, understandable to those with a wee bit of math background, is in Michael Brennen, *A Preface to Econometrics* (Cincinnati: South-Western, 1962).

Answer: What about education, age, sex, proximity to labor market areas, job experience, and job training? Given such a rough hypothetical model, the econometrician will gather data —lots of them are available in the United States—and will run what is called a "regression model." What this means is that the econometrician will test to see how strongly related black incomes are to each of the variables in the model. Somewhere along the line, most econometricians will point out that correlation, or the relationship between the variables, does not explain causation. Unfortunately, some econometricians are much less humble about their conclusions than their methodology and statistical theory tell them to be. For example, John Kain, one of the best-known American econometricians, whose work was mentioned earlier, has prefaced one study on the costs to blacks of residential discrimination (a study which was cited above) by stating: "Neither the findings of our study, nor previous analyses conclusively demonstrate the existence of a discrimination markup in urban housing markets. This may be because the theoretical and measurement problems are so great. . . . However, the preponderance of evidence points toward the presence of some markup." [11] Those of us who do not know, in terms of statistical theory, the difference between "conclusive evidence" and a "preponderance of evidence" are surely technically incapable of determining what Kain's study really has discovered, if anything. However, if you read the literature on black poverty, there are numerous occasions when similar studies are cited by writers who probably have no real understanding of the methods used. What this means is that econometricians have a ready audience because of the sophistication of their models, but an audience which cannot critically analyze econometric work, and who, by and large, accept it readily to bolster their own arguments. This is, of course, a good thing, politically speaking, as long as econometricians are on your side of the argument.

An additional limitation of this kind of analysis is that, as in

11. John Kain and John Quigley, "Housing Market Discrimination, Homeownership and Savings Behavior," Program on Regional and Urban Economics, Discussion Paper no. 58 (Cambridge: Harvard University Press, 1970), p. 8.

the work of Gary Becker, only those things which can be measured by statistical methods are taken seriously as causative variables. Thus, attempts to explain the causes of black poverty which ignore, for example, hatred and fear, and which, of necessity, assume human participants have unchanging attitudes, should be taken as tentative probability statements, at best. Basing public policy on such studies, in these times of unprecedented attitudinal change, seems to me utterly quixotic. However, even given these limitations of their models, econometricians have presented empirical verification of some of the more commonly observed features of black poverty. Also—and this bears on my later argument—econometricians, when compared with most other economists in this country, have produced some of the most informative work on black poverty.

As an example of one of the more thorough and highly publicized studies of this kind,—a study which has already had a large impact on the economics profession—let me comment once again on the following conclusions of Lester Thurow's *Poverty and Discrimination:*

1. The absolute number of poor has declined, but the gap between black income and white income, one of the best measures of the monetary costs of discrimination, has remained essentially constant. That is, the relative position of blacks in the economy has remained fixed; they are on the bottom.

2. Growth in the whole economy will reduce some poverty, and full employment will help blacks more than whites.

3. Though education is related to black income, the more education a black person gets, the smaller the proportion of the white income for similar employment he or she will be paid.

In other words, Thurow and Kain, prominent among American econometricians who are concerned with black poverty, have used their powerful techniques to confirm the arguments of others over the years that most blacks get a rotten deal from the American economic order. These econometric studies, therefore, can be added to the work of Michael Harrington and of urban anthropologists like Thomas Gladwin, to presidential commission studies like the 1968 *Report of the National Advisory Commission on Civil Disorders,* and to the work of other non-economists who have done more descriptive analyses of the same phenomena but have reached similar conclusions. One should also mention, in this context, black authors like Baldwin, Malcolm X, Ellison, Wright, and Cleaver, who begin their work with the assumption of white racism, and then vividly describe its varied effects on blacks and whites. (Indeed, because of the level of abstraction of econometric or mathematical models, I would suggest that any˜student of black poverty should preface his or her study by reading these black writers. This would protect the student from coming to think of poverty in terms of a correlation coefficient.)

What these comments about econometric studies of poverty mean is that economists like Thurow and Kain have not added anything particularly new to the debate about black poverty, but—and this is important—they have provided impressive evidence for one side of the argument about the role of racial discrimination in causing such poverty. This may be relatively unimportant in resolving the debate, but it carries the following very important implication: the position that a major impediment to ending black poverty is institutionalized discrimination calls into question the *entire economic system,* since the system allows and encourages discrimination to occur in fact, when by law and by rhetoric all of us should be granted similar opportunities to build a good life. For all its fervent idealism, Adam Smith's invisible hand, which is supposed to regulate a capitalist system to everyone's benefit, is, in essence, the result of everyone trying to do in everyone else. The logical path from Smith's invisible hand to the quite visible hand of institutionalized realism is not a difficult one to follow.

The point here is that the argument that black poverty cannot be ended without ending discrimination may well imply that it cannot be ended without major institutional change. This, of course, is a potentially revolutionary conclusion and provides a sound logical basis for the radical theory of poverty outlined in the previous chapter. Such a conclusion also raises the question: How are economists prepared to handle such unhappy implications of some of their own most highly esteemed studies? Or, to ask it differently: Why aren't there more radical economists? The following is an attempt to answer this question.

II. Is Economics a Science (as Physics Is a Science)?

Most academic economists in this country have had quite similar graduate training, and though there are an increasing number of exceptions to this rule, young economists typically will have studied the American economy in roughly the following manner: first they will be told that the economy they are to study is the market economy of the United States, characterized chiefly by private ownership of the machines and inequality in the distribution of income. In addition, since the social sciences in the twentieth century have been fragmented into separate disciplines, they will be told that economists have been left a relatively narrow range of questions to ask. Thus, most economists typically define their subject as the study of how our economy allocates our scarce resources among all the competing needs for them, *assuming the present pattern of ownership and control.*

Moreover, the young economist will be informed that the only acceptable method by which to pursue this study is the so-called scientific method. As everyone knows, what this means is that economists have learned to ape the methods used in the physical sciences whereby one attempts to understand reality by making certain assumptions about a part of reality, deducing hypotheses from these assumptions, and then testing these hypotheses against observed behavior in the real world. The chemist carefully measuring two kinds of liquid into a test tube and then recording the result of their reaction is "doing science" in the *physical* sciences. The chemist's counterpart in the *social* sciences is the economist who uses a hypothetical model of aggregate consumer behavior, together with reams of numerical data and computer facilities, to try to predict next year's total Gross National Product.

In order to emphasize how important this kind of training is in shaping the politics of American economists, it is worthwhile to discuss how social science is done and what are some rather important implications of practicing it. Ted Behr, writing with four other radical economists, has correctly defined the scientific approach as being a "dichotomization of life and knowledge, knowing and livng," that is, science is based on the notion that "there is an objective physical world with knowable laws that can be determined through various empirical testing procedures. Given knowledge of these laws and facts, man can then decide how to live. They are assumed to be separable: scientific knowledge first, then morality. . . . Many social scientists in fields other than economics also consider their goal to be the elevation of their discipline to the level of an objective science studying some aspects of human behavior." [12] Science, therefore, is, in the pure sense, nonemotional, nonsubjective, amoral, and, by itself, utterly devoid of political content. (Though, of course, one can use science as a way to study the implications of any of several competing ways to solve a particular problem.)

Behr and his friends make several criticisms of "normal science," but most concern rather technical matters in the accumulation and use of economic data, and need not detain us; what is relevant here is their suggestion that

> perhaps the most severe criticism of modern economic science [is that it] exhibits a one-dimensional emphasis on the objective mode of human experience. Science implies that man learns about his environment only through objective study. . . . Events that are still mysterious are not yet understood because they have not been adequately studied in an objective manner. . . . The kind of knowledge that arises from objective consciousness tends to be concerned more with quantity than with quality. . . . For example, engineering science told us how to make a car. Economic science measured the effect on GNP of producing ten million cars each year . . . neither science bothered to say much about the effects of the car on the quality of life.

The point here is that modern economics intentionally excludes from analysis those experiences and those possibilities which are not understandable by the strictly "objective, intellectual processes." Such an exclusion, of course, implies that the "normal scientist" may be inclined to develop a personal style of inquiry

12. This and the following quote are from Ted Behr *et al.*, "Toward a Radical Political Economics," *Review of Radical Political Economics*, July, 1971, pp. 18 and 21, respectively.

in which many normal experiences—such as love, hate, compassion, sympathy—are considered invalid guides to reality precisely because they are essentially ambiguous and certainly unmeasurable responses.

Theodore Roszak has neatly summarized this view by suggesting that it implies that "a man is a scientist not because of what he sees, but because of *how* he sees it." [13] And, of course, the scientist who believes in the possibility of "the objective conscious" will be inclined to view all alternative methodologies as incorrect. Roszak describes this point of view as follows: "Scientific knowledge is not just feeling or speculation or subjective ruminating. It is a verifiable description of reality that exists independent of any purely personal considerations. It is true . . . real . . . dependable. . . . It works. And that at least is how we define an expert: he is one who *really* knows what is what, because he cultivates an objective consciousness." [14]

To Roszak, the consequences of the pervasiveness of the "scientific culture," as he describes American society, are legion. He suggests that the "mentality of the ideal scientist becomes the very soul of the society," and we all become hardened to the "cold scientific facts" of a matter; we learn to refuse our "non-objective" selves and thus react with cold aplomb to the

> Secretary of Defense who tells the public without blinking an eye that our country possesses the "overkill" capacity to destroy any given enemy ten times . . . the high-rise glass and aluminum slab that deprives us of visual involvement by offering us only functional linearity and massive reflecting surfaces . . . the celebrated surgeon who assures us that his heart transplant was a "success" though the patient of course died. . . . [15]

To practice "normal science" is to be tempted into a personal style whereby one increasingly narrows one's range of inquiry and increasingly refuses to consider the moral implications of what one is doing.

Abraham Maslow, an eminent psychologist and philosopher of

13. Theodore Roszak, *The Making of a Counterculture* (Garden City: Doubleday, 1968), p. 213 (Roszak's emphasis).
14. *Ibid.*, p. 208.
15. *Ibid.*, p. 216.

science, has written of the "neurotic" scientist, whose personal needs become diffused in his or her scientific method, the latter becoming largely a result of the former.[16] He argues that the method of inquiry a particular person chooses to use in studying reality may tell us more about his or her psychological needs than about the reality chosen for study. This is a powerful argument which asks only that we consider the possibility that the psychological needs of the "pure" mathematician may be different from those of the "romantic" poet, remembering, of course, that *both* are trying to describe events in the real world. In other words, "science" as we know it in the twentieth century may reveal as much about our collective need to bring order to a chaotic universe than it reveals about that universe. In any case, we probably all could agree with Maslow's suggestion that

> it would be a blow to science if all scientists preferred the same problem, the same method, the same philosophy. . . . Clearly science is a collaboration, a divison of labor, and no single man is responsible for the whole of it, nor could he be. . . . No, this is not the issue. Rather it is the tendency to get pious and metaphysical about these personal preferences and to exalt them into rules for everyone else. It is the insistence on generating sweeping generalizations and excluding philosophies of knowledge, of truth, and therefore of human nature that makes trouble.[17]

And, in economics, anyway, we have trouble of precisely this kind. Modern economics—at least the kind which makes one rich, famous, and considered brilliant—is "scientific," is expressed mathematically and statistically; and the profession has increasingly closed its doors on all those who would practice a different brand of inquiry.

What is important here about these comments on economic method is the implication they have for the politics of economists. Since modern science is the practice of describing the way things work, not how they *should* work, a scientist can pass judgment on the way the world works only when *acting as a nonscientist*. And, should he or she be an especially outspoken

16. Abraham Maslow, *The Psychology of Science* (New York: Harper & Row, 1966), Chapter 4.
17. *Ibid.*, p. 57.

economist whose writings intentionally and continually take strong political positions (as, for example, John Kenneth Galbraith), he or she will be considered by many economists as a "mere" journalist, or, worse, a fuzzy sociologist. Consider for a moment how conveniently one might adopt a *cautious* position regarding the way the world "ought to be," if one is judged professionally by one's peers precisely in terms of how cautious is one's scientific research. It would be difficult, indeed, to convince your colleagues that you are an objective scientist the day after you are arrested for helping students occupy the ROTC building on your campus.

To adopt the scientific method as one's basic approach to understanding reality is to be inclined toward adopting a similarly cautious and unflamboyant political style. Of course, I cannot prove this argument by a poll, since there is no independent measure of "a cautious political style," nor of any of the other terms I have used here. I can only appeal to my reader to 1) consider the internal logic of my argument, and 2) take a look around you and see whether the argument I've made is consistent with the behavior of scientists you've known.

III. Economists and Social Class

There is more to this matter of trying to explain why so few economists are radicals, in addition to the fact that their method of inquiry inhibits a radical political style. Robert Heilbroner has suggested that an important explanaton of the paucity of radical economists has to do with what social class economists become a part of as practitioners. In discussing the fact that the "middle group" of the academic profession (associate professors) in 1967 made an average income of fourteen thousand dollars per year, while full professors (the highest grade) made an average of twenty-one thousand, Heilbroner says: "I do not see why it should be doubted that economists, like all groups, take on the values and standards of the social-economic milieu in which they live." [18] And the cause of the "irrelevance" of much

18. Robert Heilbroner and Arthur M. Ford, *Is Economics Relevant?* (Pacific Palisades, Calif.: Goodyear, 1971), p. xii.

of economics and the overcautiousness of many economists is "not the discipline of economics. . . . The fault lies rather with the reluctance of many [economists] to use their . . . skills for purposes that may be intellectually uncomfortable, or politically risky or simply out-of-step with their colleagues." [19] To paraphrase Heilbroner, the revolution is not likely to come from the top 20 percent of the income scale. As a group, economists have succeeded very nicely in carving out for themselves a relatively safe, highly-paid niche by doing science and not advocating wholesale social change. Why, one might ask, should they do anything differently? Indeed, if professional economists behave the way their models assume all others behave in a capitalist economy—that is, as income maximizers—it would clearly be "irrational" for economists to advocate change in a social order in which they get more income than the great majority of other workers.

Other writers have expanded on the "economist as part of the upper class" theme and have suggested that in addition to being rich (or perhaps because of it), economists spend much of their time serving the needs of other members of the "ruling" class. Defining economics as "value free," of course, places economists in the same kind of professional baliwick as engineers, who spend little time deciding whether a road is a "good" thing or a "bad" thing as long as it is structurally sound. Thus, like engineers, economists have developed certain tools which they believe are useful in solving real world problems. Institutions like the Pentagon, other sectors of the Federal government, and large corporations have been especially interested in these kinds of tools. Since economists are trained to determine the most efficient way to do things, and since the Pentagon, for example, needs such information, the usefulness of academically trained economists to the defense Establishment might have been predicted. Questions like "what is the cheapest way to destroy a forest in a hostile land?" are precisely the *kinds* of questions the economist as engineer has been trained to deal with (see discussion below), and thus economists have increasingly become the

19. *Ibid.*

paid servants of those who have money and power, and who need help in deciding how to use both.

Manuel Gottlieb has phrased this argument as follows: "in its American habitat economics recently has thrown all caution to the wind in its association with elite groups. It has evolved into the comfortable role of policy advisor for the upper crust . . . of the . . . foundation executives, for leading politicians, for corporate and union elite. . . ." In another passage Gottlieb makes the point even more forcefully: "To give advice one must learn to speak the same language and accept the working premises of the advisee; successful advisors learn to adapt advice to what is acceptable and feasible. Economists in recent years have become increasingly co-opted into the establishment, whose outlook, ideals, and premises they increasingly have accepted. . . . Hardly a move or strategical turn of the establishment has not been slavishly followed or rationalized by economists in its entourage." [20]

All of this is only to say that the economics practiced by American economists today is not the kind of undertaking which nurtures would-be radicals. The professional and financial advantages of spending one's time on narrow questions in economic engineering are considerable. However, even though what I have argued may partially explain why so few economists advocate "radical" or "revolutionary" change, it doesn't explain what kind of system they do advocate. As it turns out, they are typically "for capitalism," and the fact of their allegiance to a particular system invokes a further question: How can objective social scientists, who claim they study their subject with utter dispassion, so consistently become defenders of the system they study? What follows is one possible answer.

IV. Economics and the Cult of Efficiency

Given their own definition of their subject and method, economists have confined their inquiry to two kinds of basic theoreti-

20. Manuel Gottlieb, "Mukerjee: Economics Become Social Science," *Journal of Economic Issues*, December, 1971, pp. 45–46.

cal questions. The first question—How does the system operate as a whole?—has been answered, at least in part, by the Keynesian revolution and its afterthoughts. The second question— How do the subsectors of the aggregate economy (the labor markets, the consumers, the firms, etc.) operate has brought to fruition a tremendously large group of theories which collectively are called microeconomics. Microeconomic models are typically more oversimplified, more mathematical in exposition, and, in my judgment, significantly less successful than macroeconomic models in explaining much about our economy. This limitation is the result not so much of the questions asked by microeconomists but of the particularly feeble methods they use in attempting to find answers.

In building such models, microeconomists usually confine their efforts to the pages of such journals as the *American Economic Review*, a quaint periodical ordinarily containing mathematical models understandable to only a portion of the economic profession and totally incomprehensible to almost everyone else. Not surprisingly, the president of the United States more frequently consults his economic advisors about their macroeconomic models than he does about, say, their latest micromodel which assumes a two-commodity world, without history or politics, and occupied by two sexless people, without race or philosophy, one the owner of a business, the other a consumer.[21]

What is important here is that in doing both "macro" and "micro" economic analysis, economists assimilate certain attitudes about the system they are studying. In essence, conventional economic theory provides a *built-in* value system which can be generalized simply as follows: The system to be studied —the existing economy of this country—is to be judged primar-

21. If these comments seem harsh, look at, for example, the March, 1970, issue of the *American Economic Review* and ask yourself if these economists are talking about the world you live in or about one they have constructed for their own private use. This issue of the *AER* contained no articles which dealt directly with the Vietnam war, black poverty, white poverty, environmental pollution, urban congestion, or the military-industrial syndrome, and utterly no hint emerges from the issue that things are amiss in this land. A strange world, indeed!

ily in terms of one criterion, efficiency. Now, "efficiency," as understood by economists, means: Given limited natural and human resources, and assuming more goods are always better than less, how do we maximize the real net value of total output of goods and services? This is, pure and undefiled, the prevailing value system about the economy shared by most economists in this country, and even a cursory glance at their published literature will prove this claim beyond doubt. For example, consider the following statement by Paul Samuelson (whose textbook, or one of the many others patterned closely after it, has probably been used by the great majority of American economists in beginning economics courses). He puts the matter straightforwardly: "We study [competitive pricing] for the light it throws on efficient organization of the economy's resources. The pathology of interference with supply and demand helps to bring out the remarkable efficiencies produced by perfect competition." And in a later passage about whether a monopoly is "a good or bad thing" Samuelson puts it most succinctly: "Any *haphazard* interference with competitive supply and demand is likely—save in some exceptional circumstances—to be a bad thing rather than a good thing." [22] It is interesting to note that Samuelson calls interference with "efficiency" pathological, thus identifying "inefficiency" and "noncompetitiveness" with disease.

H. H. Liebhafsky, one of the more perceptive of American economists writing on this issue, has pointed out quite clearly the major implication of Samuelson's argument. As Liebhafsky puts it, "to argue that a particular configuration of prices *should* exist is tantamount to arguing that the social order which will produce that configuration *should* exist." [23] In other words, to praise the efficiency of competitive pricing is to praise the *status quo* in a competitive economy. And, quite obviously, such implicit praise is clearly inconsistent with the "economist as scientist" image which Samuelson has exemplified throughout his career. [24]

22. Paul Samuelson, *Economics*, 6th ed. (New York: McGraw-Hill, 1967), pp. 378–379 (Samuelson's emphasis).

23. H. H. Liebhafsky, *American Government and Business* (New York: Wiley, 1971), p. 15 (Liebhafsky's emphasis).

24. In all fairness, it should be pointed out that Samuelson prefaces his textbook with a lengthy discussion of the impossibility of "perfect objectiv-

Because of this fetish of efficiency, American economists typically spend most of their time figuring out ways to make the existing system work "better," and by this they mean more productively, either in part or in the aggregate. Now, a second and extremely important feature of this built-in value system is the heroic, yet unproved, assumption that the competitive market system is the most productive one imaginable consistent with political democracy, the second major part of the American Creed.[25] Thus—and this logical sequence is a crucial one—if the most efficient system is the best, and capitalism is the most efficient consistent with an assumed political system, *ipso facto*, capitalism is the best system.

In some of the theoretical and descriptive literature it is mentioned that besides being the most efficient system, capitalism, also maximizes choice, or, more generally, freedom—economic *and* political. But ordinarily this advantage of capitalism over its alternatives is assumed without being mentioned, perhaps because "freedom" is a concept which does not lend itself well to mathematical and theoretical analysis. Furthermore, if capitalism *is* the most efficient system, and if it is assumed to maximize freedom, then, by definition, an efficient system is a free one. A notable exception in this regard is Milton Friedman, who has for years explicitly and loudly proclaimed that "freedom" is the most important by-product of competitive capitalism, and that it is precisely for this reason that he advocates such a system.[26] Of course, any such argument about the relationship between the economy and freedom is subjective, since it depends entirely on how one defines "freedom."

The point is that the main corpus of economic theory is characterized by an inherent faith in the market system as the most efficient—thus the best—system. And the typical American

ity" in economics; nonetheless, he has been pre-eminent among those American economists who have used the "objective" stance while championing the cause of the American capitalist system. For an especially good discussion of the "objectivity" of Paul Samuelson's economics, see Hugh Stretton, *The Political Sciences* (New York: Basic Books, 1969), pp. 346–352.

25. See Liebhafsky, especially Chapters 1 and 2, and the Appendix.

26. Milton Friedman, *Capitalism and Freedom* (Chicago: University of Chicago Press, 1962), especially Chapter 1.

economist has been trained to appreciate the elegant workings of a market economy which, incidentally, he or she ordinarily participates in as a member of the upper middle class. These two factors, combined with an acquired taste for posing as a dispassionate observer of the social order, predispose American economists toward a life of political moderation—that is, political liberalism.

A much more strident and rhetorical version of my argument regarding the stance of orthodox economists is the following statement made by a group of radical academic economists to the officers of the American Economic Association in December, 1969:

> We have come to denounce the A. E. A. Economists in the U.S. work as a group and work contrary to the interests of the masses of people. . . . Economists are the sycophants of inequality, alienation, destruction of environment, imperialism, racism, and the subjugation of women. . . . They preach the gospel of rational efficiency, justifying the reduction of man and nature to marketable commodities. . . . All they tell us about the war in Vietnam is how to fight it more efficiently; they apply mathematical models to "prove" that foreign investment helps the development of poor countries; they tell us that racism is the result of "personal preference"; they tell us that private property and wage differentials present a system of personal material incentives "necessary" for "growth." . . . They show how to manipulate people so that the system's hinges are smoothly oiled. Economists . . . develop "people appeasement" programs to prevent rebellion; when a reactionary government controls a poor country, economists are set to "rationalize" and "stabilize." . . . The A. E. A. economists have chosen to serve the status quo. We have chosen to fight it.[27]

This passage makes the distinction between liberal and radical economic analyses rather explicitly.

In any case, by maintaining faith in the adequacy of liberal reform, economists can avoid considering the possibility that such measures will, like all their predecessors, end up by failing

27. Printed in *Newsletter*, Union of Radical Political Economics, Winter, 1970, pp. 1–2.

to deal with the main problem, a problem that their graduate training has perhaps not prepared them for. That is, the problem of black poverty, for example, may indeed arise from the basic nature of the *whole system,* in the sense that black poverty, or any poverty, can simply not be solved unless we change some basic features of the modern American economy. The drawback of such an unhappy conclusion is, of course, that it contradicts the value system, which most economists maintain, that competitive capitalism is the best system.

I suggested earlier that several econometricians (especially Kain and Thurow) have provided sophisticated empirical support for the argument that the root cause of black poverty is discrimination, or institutional racism. What "institutional racism" means in this context, of course, is that even if black incomes are moved up to some minimum level, the most obnoxious features of the system will remain. Poor blacks with a five-thousand-dollar guaranteed minimum income, or whatever, would still have to pay higher prices, would still receive inadequate public services, would still have to send their children to financially poorer schools, still would be unable to buy a house in any neighborhood they might choose, and would still, for the most part, be confined to a ghetto, only slightly improved. In addition, virtually no change in the overall control of the system would be bought about by guaranteed income legislation: whites would still own and control the productive equipment of the economy, even in areas which are predominantly black; whites would also continue to make most of the laws and would still run the schools, the cities, and the counties; and a white man, perhaps one elected by appealing to the racism in us all, would still be in the White House.

V. A Summing Up

Let me sum up the two threads of my argument in this chapter so that what follows will make some sense. First, I suggested that many studies of black poverty, including some of the most impressive economic ones, have shown that discrimination against blacks must be overcome before the problem can be solved. I suggested that this could well call for more than minor changes in the economic system. Second, I have tried to show that economists are ill-equipped to handle such problems since their training typically leads to a timid political style, buttressed by a strong faith in market capitalism, and this implies a jaundiced view toward real change in that system. Thus, I have tried to demonstrate the serious contradiction between the policy implications of economic studies of black poverty and the value system economists assimilate in being trained as professionals.

The point of all this has been an attempt to tie together some of the more subtle implications of the previous two chapters and to provide a transition to the analyses of political responses to urban poverty which follow. It has been necessary to go through this methodological chapter in order to demonstrate why such a great majority of academic economists (and other social scientists) have developed and lent support to liberal antipoverty programs. Hopefully this chapter will also provide understanding about how the failure of liberal reform over the years to end urban poverty has caused many young economists to break away from the old methods—even though they were trained in these methods—and adopt a "radical" stance in the profession.

I have now described the problem, discussed its causes, and sought to explain why economists have divided themselves into two basically different camps regarding what should be done to solve urban poverty. I trust that by now the stage has been set to talk about policy.

Chapter Four

LIBERAL REMEDIES FOR URBAN POVERTY

What are the various antipoverty efforts which are based on the assumption that poverty can be eliminated in a mature industrial capitalist system? The answer to this question is best prefaced by a discussion of two aspects of the liberal position which have been hinted at earlier, but which need further integration into the theme of this book. The first aspect concerns "pluralism," a component of the liberal position which derives from modern political theory; the second is the relationship between urban poverty and the transformation of American agriculture during the past few decades.

I. Pluralism and American Liberalism

Let me discuss the political element first. During the past twenty years or so American political scientists, buttressed by data and model-building in sociology and economics, have developed a thory of the political system called "pluralism." According to this view, the more heterogeneous a social system is, the greater will be the number of groups which, in order to protect their own economic, political, religious, and other interests, will organize politically and assert themselves as viable elements in the political scene. An example of this kind of model-building will indicate the essential features of the pluralist argument. Consider the argument developed by John Kenneth Galbraith in *American Capitalism: The Concept of Countervailing Power,* written in 1952.[1]

According to Galbraith, the development of one large, powerful political-economic sector—for example, large industrial firms operating in concert—will create, on the other side of the market, the need and the energy for the emergence of equally large and powerful sectors—for example, labor unions. Laborers will organize in order to protect their interests in conflicts with big businesses. The conflicts between these two rivals, and the enormous impact their efforts have on the rest of society, will bring into being ever-larger government units, especially at the Federal level, since the impact of big business and big labor is national in scale. In other words, one principal conclusion of the pluralist argument is that the development of government reflects the divergent needs of all these various power blocs, checks their growth, and arbitrates differences between them. Other pluralist models are similar in their general characteristics. For example, the pluralist explanation of politics in a single community would be that they embody the result of all the competing interests groups in that community and the group efforts to protect interests from encroachment by other groups. What is especially important here is the clear implication of the pluralist position that the government, at whatever level, is considered the "best" and the "legitimate" arbitrator of the conflicting needs of the community. The implementation of laws, therefore, is assumed to result in a continually evolving set of relationships, reflecting at any given time some element, however small, of all the competing, organized groups within that governmental unit.[2]

1. Boston: Houghton-Mifflin, 1952.
2. I have been advised by Phil Green that the best theoretical statement of the pluralist position is Robert Dahl, *A Preface to Democratic Theory*

The principal policy implication of pluralism is, assuredly, quite pedestrian: if you have problems, organize and enter into politics at that level of government where your problem can best be solved. This primary implication is also quite consistent with all that has been said here about the basic character of the liberal reform position concerning social policy. It is also clear how precisely this model fits the needs of those committed to the assumption that social problems *must* be resolved within the framework of existing social institutions. If the poor have problems—such as too little income—it is through legitimate government, with legitimate political efforts, that their problems are best to be solved.

Of course, critics of pluralist thought—C. Wright Mills (author of *The Power Elite*), Baran and Sweezy (*Monopoly Capital*), Ferdinand Lundberg (*The Rich and the Super-Rich*), William Domhoff (who has written about the ruling elite in his books *The Higher Circles* and *Who Rules America?*),[3] and others—simply deny its basic argument that America is ruled by untold numbers of competing interest groups. Mills's "power elite," Lundberg's "super-rich," and Baran and Sweezy's "monopoly capitalists" are terms implying that America is ruled by an oligarchy of very powerful individuals and the organizations they control. An obvious implication of this antipluralist position is that a government controlled by the rich and those who serve their interests cannot be counted upon to deal adequately with the problems of those who are of other classes, who live in other neighborhoods, and whose welfare may be either beside the point or inimical to the interests of the rich. Thus an antipluralist would reasonably deduce that *fundamental* political and social change, rather than maintenance of the existing political structure, is necessary to serve the interests of *some* groups in our social order. In short, pluralism, a major intellectual cor-

(Chicago: University of Chicago Press, 1956). For a more well-known application of pluralist theory, see Arnold Rose, *The Power Structure* (New York: Oxford University Press, 1967).

3. C. Wright Mills, *The Power Elite* (New York: Oxford University Press, 1956); Ferdinand Lundberg, *The Rich and the Super-Rich* (New York: Bantam, 1968); G. William Domhoff, *The Higher Circles* (New York: Random House, 1971); and Domhoff, *Who Rules America?* (Englewood Cliffs: Prentice-Hall, 1967).

nerstone of modern liberal thought, is, of course, more useful as a view of reality the less one is interested in significant change in American social institutions.

II. Agricultural Modernization and Urban Poverty

Regarding the historical roots of contemporary urban poverty, it has been argued persuasively by Frances Fox Piven and Richard Cloward (see my Acknowledgements) that this poverty is primarily the result of two important historical factors: 1) the long-term technological transformation of the United States economy, and 2) the short-run collapse in total production in the 1930's.[4] These two elements of our history have played quite important roles in determining both the character of urban poverty and the ways we have tried to handle it as a social problem.

Relief for the indigent has, of course, been a constant preoccupation of reformers throughout human history, for most communities have had poor people. The United States is no exception to this rule, and all our cities, from our inception as a nation, have had their ladies' aid societies, their church handout programs, and similar efforts to minimize the suffering of the poor (without significantly changing power or wealth relationships), while, simultaneously and importantly, assuaging the guilt of the rich. It must have been a good deal easier to drive to church on Sunday from the mansion if on Saturday one had spent the day knitting mittens for poor people.

Interestingly enough, this kind of relief was the principal type in this country until very recent times, though there were some local communities and a few states which did try to implement small-scale, usually half-hearted, public attempts to alleviate the plight of the poor. And it might have stayed that way but for the emergence of two great "relief explosions," to use the

4. Frances Fox Piven and Richard Cloward, *Regulating the Poor: The Functions of Public Welfare* (New York: Random House, 1971), especially Chapters 1 and 7. The discussion in this section follows the argument in their book fairly closely.

image provided by Piven and Cloward. These explosions were too large for private charity and too threatening to be ignored by Federal and state politicians. The first significant expansion of the welfare rolls was the direct result of the Great Depression of the 1930's. It is an indication of how little government had concerned itself with the poor that public aid—welfare expenditures—amounted to only sixty million dollars in 1929. However, things changed dramatically soon after because of the increasing intensity of the Depression. By 1932, there were over fifteen million people unemployed (about 25 percent of the labor force), and by 1935, over *twenty million people* were on relief.[5] Consequently, total expenditures for welfare rose to about three billion dollars in 1934–35 (a 5,000 percent increase since 1929).[6]

Most of the programs initiated in the 1930's to deal with such massive income transfers were financially similar to contemporary ones: they were paid for in part by the Federal government and in part by the states, and they were administered locally. During this decade the relief program was extended into what we currently think of as "social security": for example, programs were added to take care of workers when they retired or became disabled, unemployment insurance was provided to give temporary relief to those out of work, and public housing was built for the "submerged middle class," a convenient term for the middle-class and lower-middle-class unemployed who had been displaced temporarily, it was assumed, by the Depression. Predictably, World War II, which ultimately ended the Depression, also terminated this first great relief explosion. As war industries grew apace along with the war effort, most of the unemployed were put back on the job. The remainder were a relatively small number of the permanently poor: old people, sick people, and others who could not perform a job if they got one. By 1945 total government expenditures on welfare had fallen to one billion dollars.[7]

The second great relief explosion, according to Piven and

5. *Ibid.*, p. 75.
6. Ida C. Merriam, "Social Welfare Expenditures, 1929–1967," *Social Security Bulletin*, December, 1967, p. 5.
7. *Ibid.*

Cloward, resulted from the "economic convulsion in agriculture," which is "the key to an understanding of the turbulence of the 1960's, and to a full understanding of the contemporary welfare explosion." [8] What is especially important about this convulsion is that it reached a frenetic apex in relatively recent times, especially after 1945. For example, the average number of tractors per farm—a convenient index of technological change on farms —doubled between 1945 and 1964. Moreover, modernization helped encourage farmers to buy and operate ever-larger farms; "between 1950 and 1969, *one million* farms disappeared, the 3 million remaining farms averaged . . . 30 per cent larger than the average farm ten years earlier." [9] Naturally, the most important by-product of this technological revolution in farming was the decreasing need for agricultural labor. Piven and Cloward quote a Presidential Commission on Rural Poverty which found that between 1950 and 1965 "new machines and new methods increased farm output in the United States by 45% and reduced farm employment by 45%." [10] What this means is that in the space of fifteen years, the number of farm employees necessary for producing the nation's growing agricultural output had fallen by one-half. Among other effects of modernization was a great migration from farms to urban areas: since 1940 over twenty million people have moved from farms to the cities, and more than four million have been black.[11]

Thus, by the 1960's, the effects on urban areas of what had happened on the farm were becoming increasingly obvious. The striking change in the number of people on relief during the 1960's is indicative. The number of families receiving AFDC [12] funds more than doubled during the 1960's, though it had increased by only 17 percent during the 1950's; and in New York

8. Piven and Cloward, p. 200.
9. *Ibid.*, pp. 200–201. (Emphasis added.)
10. *Ibid.*, p. 201.
11. *Ibid.*
12. AFDC (Aid for Dependent Children) is implemented by the Social Security Administration and was, for most of the early years of its existence, used to supplement the income of widowed women with children. Increasingly, however, the AFDC funds are paid to deserted women with children and to unwed mothers.

and California the rise during the 1960's was even greater than
the national average, with most of the increase occurring after
1965.[13] Total government expenditures on public aid to the poor
also increased greatly during the decade: [14]

1960	$4.1 billion
1965	6.3
1967	8.8
1968	11.1
1969	13.2
1970	16.1 (preliminary estimate)

There have been several different explanations of why the
number of people on relief changed so dramatically during the
1960's, especially after 1965. Again, let me quote Piven and Cloward on the essential causes of this "dramatic increase." In sum-
ming up their argument they state:

> . . . Modernization, migration, urban unemployment, the
> breakup of families, rising grant levels, and other factors contrib-
> uted to a growing pool of "eligible" families in the 1950's and
> 1960's. Nevertheless, the relief rolls did not rise until the 1960's.
> And when they did, it was largely as a result of governmental
> programs designed to moderate widespread political unrest
> among black poor. One consequence of these programs was that
> the poor were suddenly to apply for relief in unprecedented
> numbers (except in the South); another . . . was that welfare of-
> ficials were suddenly stimulated to approve applications in un-
> precedented numbers. The terms in which that crisis must be ex-
> plained are economic disruption, large scale migration, mass
> volatility and electoral responses—a sequence of disturbances
> leading to a precipitous expansion of the relief rolls.[15]

In other words, the combination of agricultural modernization
and federal efforts to avoid the rebellion of the urban poor put
pressure on local welfare officials to add unprecedented numbers of people to the rolls. This growth in the rolls occurred especially *after* the clear threat to stability evidenced by the
urban riots from 1964 on.

13. Piven and Cloward, Source Table I, p. 350.
14. Taken from *Statistical Abstract of the United States*, 1971, p. 271.
15. Piven and Cloward, p. 338.

A major implication of this argument should be considered very carefully, for it is utterly *at odds with any theory of urban poverty which assumes that the urban poor are "different" from you and me in their unwillingness to provide for themselves if given ample opportunity.* Try to imagine yourself in the following position: Forget all but the most fundamental reading and writing skills, forget all the technological skills you have learned as a middle-class college student, forget all your personal contacts in the area to which you are going to move (except for a few relatives who are unemployed, or struggling not to be), give up all your money and luxuries, give up your car, take on the responsibility of a child or two, then go to some distant city a thousand miles away, and see how you fare. Try to imagine also how long it will be before you might seek directions to the local welfare office.

These relationships between contemporary urban poverty and the modernization of agriculture are important, for they are a good part of the reason that the liberal approach to antipoverty is couched, to a significant degree, in moral terms. The liberal sees the urban poor as having been victimized by factors largely outside their control; liberal strategies to abolish poverty, therefore, are based upon both economic (and other social-science) theories and a *moral judgment* about the injustice done to the poor. This, of course, gives a special character to liberal efforts, and gives rise to a special kind of indignation when such programs are criticized, or when they fail. It is important to note the difference between the liberal's approach, in this context, and that of the conservative, using the contemporary American political meaning of that term. The latter most frequently views the urban poor as being the main cause of their own plight, and thus the conservative's program to combat poverty is ordinarily a simple indifference, buttressed by occasional suggestions, for example, in the case of Banfield, about how best to maintain law, order, and civility in poor neighborhoods.[16]

In any case, from the liberal perspective, the contemporary

16. Edward Banfield, *The Unheavenly City* (Boston: Little, Brown, 1970), Chapter 11.

urban poor are poor because they typically have migrated to cities where the demand for labor at their level of skill is simply not adequate to give them all jobs, although the market provided low-skilled jobs to white immigrants in the nineteenth and early twentieth centuries. The liberal sees the poor as victimized by the transformation of the rural economy, victimized by the lack of jobs in the economically stagnant central city they invariably move to, victimized by the transportation system which makes it difficult for them to get to the good jobs. Finally—but, to the liberal, most important—in spite of all these problems, the poor person's plight is subject to great improvement through ordinary political means, by reform of key social institutional arrangements in the city and national economy. This perspective has resulted in the antipoverty program outlined below.

III. The Liberal Antipoverty Program

To begin with, there are four general aspects of the liberal reform program: 1) those antipoverty measures concerned with the labor market, the demand for jobs, and the personal characteristics of the laborers; 2) those measures concerned with welfare payments to the unemployable and the employed poor; 3) those concerned with trying to change the "culture of poverty"; and 4) programs aimed at minimizing discrimination. I shall first review these different parts of the liberal's program and then evaluate the results of liberal reform and a few implications of these results.

THE LABOR MARKET [17]

Maintaining Full Employment Interestingly enough, probably the single most important element of the liberal antipoverty pro-

17. Excluded here is a discussion of the minimum wage laws, which reform liberals of yesteryear fought for successfully. I have not included the minimum wage as a part of contemporary liberal policy because it has fallen into disrepute among many liberals, especially economists. There is a good deal of evidence to indicate that one result of minimum wage laws is increased unemployment, either because employers cut production and lay

gram is Federal monetary and fiscal policy which attempts to control the size of the national economy. The reason for this is fairly apparent: when the economy booms, tight labor markets will draw into the working force at rising wages more and more of those deemed "unemployable" before the boom. Similarly, at the first sign of recession, the low-skilled, marginal part of the labor force—the group called the "submerged middle class" in the 1930's—are the first to lose their jobs. One study mentioned above, Lester Thurow's econometric study of poverty, showed that a 1 percent increase in the number of full-time workers in a state would reduce that state's poverty rate by 0.54 percent. This means that, at any given time, a significant determinant of poverty is the inadequate demand for the products produced from the labor of mostly low-skilled workers.

The relationship between the demand for labor and the national economy has long been recognized by economists. However, since about 1955 there has been a running debate between most American economists concerning the extent to which some of the poor are actually employable, no matter how big the national economy grows. One argument suggests that there are "pockets of poverty" in the nation—parts of the ghetto, some rural areas—where there is a virtual insensitivity to the level of aggregate demand. The "culture of poverty" argument discussed earlier as a foundation-stone of liberal theories of urban poverty implies the existence of such pockets.

This side of the debate, discussed briefly in Chapter 1, is the "structuralist" position, the term implying that the way the economy is organized—and structured—makes it impossible for some people to compete: some are unskilled or uneducated, some are the wrong color, some the wrong sex, some are sick,

---

off workers when wages are forced up by government fiat, or because employers substitute machinery for the more expensive workers. The possibility of unemployment resulting from minimum wage laws is especially strong in marginal, low-wage, low-profit industries, precisely where the poor are likely to be working. For a representative discussion of the issue, and a good bibliography, see Jacob Kaufman and Terry Foran, "The Minimum Wage and Poverty," in James G. Scoville, ed., *Perspectives on Poverty and Income Distribution* (Lexington, Mass.: Heath, 1971), pp. 219–238.

and so on. On the other side of the argument are the "expansionists," whose basic conclusion is that *no* labor market, however isolated, is ultimately insensitive to aggregate demand if that demand gets *high enough.* In other words, if businesses can sell their goods at inflated prices because of growing aggregate demand, it will ultimately become profitable to them to hire all those they had thought too costly in the past: the untrained, who will have to be trained; the unschooled, who will have to be taught to read and write; the blacks, who will have to be endured; the women, who will have to be trained *and* endured. There are, in fact, many economists in the expansionist school who argue that creating full employment in the national economy is perhaps the only really effective way to eliminate absolute poverty.[18] What is important here is that both schools would agree that a full-employment economy is a necessary ingredient of any successful antipoverty program. And this part of the argument to which both sides agree has become the basis of the liberal antipoverty programs.

To demonstrate the relationship between the macroeconomy and the unemployment rate, let me briefly review the results of President Nixon's macroeconomic policy since coming to office. Recently compiled data underscore how importantly a depressed economy can affect poor people, especially those in urban areas. During his first term in office, Nixon has pursued a number of domestic economic policies; of these, especially important in the present context are his antipoverty policies and his anti-inflation measures. Regarding the former, his efforts have unquestionably intensified the problem: he has postponed his revenue-sharing program, which would have rechanneled Federal taxes to states and to cities; he has postponed welfare reform; he vetoed a massive child care bill, easily voted through Congress; and he has developed an antipoverty stance which, in essence, amounts to little more than increased surveillance of the poor. How harmful these actions have been to poor people is revealed by census data indicating that the number of urban

18. An especially strong statement of this position is in Edwin Dale, Jr., "The Great Unemployment Fallacy," *New Republic,* September 5, 1964, pp. 10–12.

poor people, as computed by the Federal government, actually increased by about 800,000 in 1971, reversing a downward trend which had extended back to at least 1959.

The president's future plans may be even bleaker. The nation's "big-city-mayors," in commenting upon Nixon's budget for the 1973 fiscal year, alleged that the budget ". . . would reduce major urban programs by $765 million in the fiscal year beginning July 1st." According to their spokesman, Henry Maier of Milwaukee, "the actual appropriations available in fiscal 1972 for urban renewal, water and sewer, open space, public housing and rental assistance for apartments is $2.4 billion, while the Administration's proposed level for fiscal 1973 is only $1.65 billion—a $765 million reduction." [19] Though all this may be number-juggling by the mayors (nobody really knows *exactly* how much the Federal government spends on anything), these local officials are certainly not wrong in stating that, to this point (August, 1972), Nixon has not seemed overly concerned about city problems.

In addition to his fainthearted efforts to end poverty, President Nixon's initial efforts to stem inflation, which failed because the macroeconomic theory on which they were based was either wrong, poorly implemented, or both, amounted to various attempts to control the price level by allowing unemployment to increase. While the unemployment rate in 1968 and 1969 was about 3.5 percent of the civilian labor force, it increased to 4.9 percent in 1970 and 6.0 percent in 1971.[20] Naturally, when unemployment increases, poverty increases, and all the other problems of the low-skilled, uneducated elements of the working force are exacerbated. The point is that Nixon's anti-inflation program in 1969 and 1970 was implemented *primarily* at the expense of the poor people, and it hurt the black poor disproportionately. Figures on unemployment for 1969–71 reveal quite clearly how serious a problem a recession is for all workers, and how much more serious it is for blacks than for whites. Consider these data: [21]

19. *New York Times,* January 26, 1972, p. 32c.
20. *Federal Reserve Bulletin,* January, 1972.
21. *Monthly Labor Review,* January, 1972. Such relative indifference to the problems of the poor as these figures reveal doubtless derives from the

Unemployment (Civilian Labor Force)

	First Quarter, 1969	Third Quarter, 1971
Blacks	6.2%	10.1%
Whites	3.0%	5.5%

This review of Nixon's policies at least indicates that the economist's argument about the strong relationship between the health of the macroeconomy and the plight of poor people is largely correct.

Manpower Programs   It should be apparent that even if the national economy is booming, there will still be problems for poor people, first because there is surely some structural unemployment, and second because even when everyone has jobs, many jobs do not pay a wage above the poverty line. Data presented earlier showed that a full *fourth* of those who are classified as "urban poor" work full time. Thus, in addition to programs for maintaining full employment in the national economy in the liberal antipoverty scheme, there are a great number of programs aimed at upgrading the skills of those who work but don't make enough money, and those who cannot work at all because they have no marketable skills. These kinds of policies are, in general, known as "manpower programs," and most of them are probably familiar ones.

What may be surprising is that the bulk of them are relatively new. Indeed, it was not until the early 1960's, with the War on Poverty,[22] that such programs began to flourish. (In 1961, Fed-

---

fact that Nixon, like most political conservatives in the United States, ultimately considers the problems of the poor to be their own fault. But, of course, trying to predict Mr. Nixon's future course of action is a precarious art. He is a politician who has been elected to public office for the past twenty-five years by campaigning against precisely those domestic economic proposals and foreign policies which he currently is implementing as president—so who knows when he may change his "fundamental philosophy" about the poor also?

22. Throughout this chapter I frequently refer to most of the antipoverty programs, ranging from New Deal public housing laws to the War on Poverty Head Start Program, without describing in detail how these programs function. I neglect these details here because I assume most of my readers will have acquired this information in some other context. For those still a

eral expenditures on manpower programs were $250 million; by 1969, they had risen to $2.5 billion.) What happened in the 1960's, in large part because of the success of the Democrats in the national election, was a genuine shift of emphasis in the entire antipoverty effort. Since, in recent years, Democrats have been elected by the working class, ethnic minorities, and intellectuals, it was not surprising that the War on Poverty was aimed primarily at relieving the problems of the working-class poor and that its programs were based on antipoverty measures influenced by academic social scientists.[23] Thus, in the Johnson

bit unsure about the difference between, for example, the Job Corps and Community Action Agencies, see the following excellent book, which explains all these programs: Joseph Kershaw, *Government Against Poverty* (Washington, D.C.: Brookings Institution, 1970). One detail ought to be given here, however, because it lends clarity to the argument. In 1964, Congress passed, and President Johnson signed, the Economic Opportunity Act, and created the Office of Economic Opportunity (OEO) to administer the programs financed by the Act. According to Johnson, the term "War on Poverty" came from a ranch meeting of Johnson and his aides, who tried, by using a metaphor familiar to Americans, to indicate how serious an effort his antipoverty program was going to be when compared to others. The early "poverty warriors" frequently emphasized the word *opportunity* in trying to distinguish the 1964 program from simple income maintenance programs. Actually, I use the term "War on Poverty" in this chapter to refer more generally to Federal antipoverty programs throughout the 1964–68 Johnson Administration, many of which have been administered by agencies other than the OEO. Federal funds for War on Poverty programs have been as follows during the past few years:

1967	$1.7 billion
1968	1.8 billion
1969	1.95 billion
1970	1.94 billion

23. This point is made explicit in Thomas Gladwin, *Poverty, U.S.A.* (Boston: Little, Brown, 1967), p. 175; however, the general conclusion that current antipoverty programs are based heavily on the efforts of social scientists emerges clearly if one reads their essays and books on the matter over the past few decades and compares their "policy" arguments to the programs which have actually been implemented. Others have argued that, at least in the short run, the basic nature of the Johnson antipoverty programs depended largely on political considerations, especially those of the national Democratic party (see Piven and Cloward, pp. 248ff). My point is only that the strong correlation between the War on Poverty and modern social science research is too strong to be the result of chance. Johnson may have forged his program to win votes in the city and calm down civil disorder, but the *way* he chose to do so depended significantly on social theory such as the culture of poverty argument. For Johnson's view, see his *Vantage Point* (New York: Holt, Rinehart and Winston, 1971), Chapter 4.

Administration, the liberal program on poverty was given full consideration, and central to that program were efforts to up-grade the skills of the poor through a great variety of manpower programs. There were the Neighborhood Youth Corps and the Job Corps, aimed at providing young dropouts with skills and, most importantly, with the right attitudes consistent with employment; and there were the JOB and CEP programs (Job Opportunities in Business and Concentrated Employment Program), whereby local industry and communities were subsidized to train and employ the unskilled. Most of these programs followed on the heels of the 1962 Manpower Development and Training Act, a broad-based effort to coordinate and make more extensive the whole network of job placement and job training in labor markets all over the country.

In general, these recent policies concerned with the labor market have tried to do two things: first, they have tried to assure an adequate aggregate demand by maintaining full employment in the national economy; second, they have tried to assure that, as the national economy grew, the poor would be able, through the various manpower training acts, to step into jobs as they became available.[24]

PUBLIC ASSISTANCE

The second major element of the liberal antipoverty program has been to extend the benefits available to those on relief, most of whom are not employable. The initial Federal and state relief programs of the thirties,[25] with their provisions for unemployment compensation and for benefits to the old, the sick, the tem-

24. For a review of the programs, see Research and Policy Committee, *Training and Jobs for the Urban Poor* (New York: Committee on Economic Development, 1970).

25. Many of the programs were initiated by the first Social Security legislation in 1935. That legislation created two kinds of programs, one for those who would contribute tax payments in advance of benefits (such as Old Age and Survivor's Benefits), and the other for those who were given public aid (such as ADFC). Our concentration here is on the latter kind of program. For an excellent review of the "old" and "new" welfare systems see Theodore F. Lowi, *The End of Liberalism* (New York: Norton, 1969), Chapter 8.

porarily disabled, and dependent children, have been extended over the years. In the 1960's, a major expansion was the Medicare program (at the Federal level, for old people) and Medicaid (at the state level, for low-income people regardless of age). Also, over the years there have been a variety of food subsidy programs for schoolchildren and for people on welfare, the latest being the Food Stamp Program, initiated in 1961.

The Congress, in passing these public assistance laws, has always had them implemented at the state level and, in some instances, by local governments. The purpose of this practice is to allow the programs to be implemented "where the problem is," and, more importantly, to tie the amount of Federal aid to the amount of aid expended by the state. Thus, the Federal government will subsidize a state's unemployment compensation program, depending on the willingness of the state to put up its own receipts. What has resulted, of course, is the patchwork national public assistance program, where the benefits one receives depends largely on where one is located. Since each state can determine the basic features of its own program, the level of the payment, the willingness to make its programs work, the dignity afforded the poor who participate in the program, and a host of other factors depend almost exclusively on politicians and bureaucrats at all the different levels of state and local governments.

Needless to say, there are several severe weaknesses in the public assistance program. First, there are the great differences among the benefits received. An AFDC family of four in Mississippi, for example, received maximum monthly payments in 1968 of $66 from state and Federal assistance, while its counterpart in Massachusetts received a maximum of $332. Second, in addition to the fundamental unfairness in the way the program is administered, it has been weakened because it is the final result of so many different laws, is administered by so many different bureaucracies, and is subject to the whims of so many individuals in the various state and local governments. Thus, there has been a clamor for new laws, especially for a single measure which will make obsolete the hodgepodge which is the present public-assistance program. The failure of the New Deal legislation, therefore, has been the origin of several "negative income tax" programs, one of which was actually introduced into Congress in 1970 (and a similar bill was passed by the House Ways and Means Committee in March, 1972). This program was the major part of President Nixon's welfare reform program and shared with all its counterparts several important characteristics. These "guaranteed annual income" programs are attempts to institute one annual payment to all families, subject to their willingness to accept work in the public or private sector if it is available. Built into each, of course, is a particular level of income which will be available to every family (if its breadwinner has been willing to work at jobs offered).

In the latest Nixon plan (1971), this level is about twenty-two hundred dollars for a family of four. The Nixon plan would take the place of most public assistance programs, including food stamps and other food subsidies. The two most important characteristics of the Nixon guaranteed annual income plan should be mentioned: 1) It ties benefits to employment, in the sense that it is designed especially for the "working poor." Those persons able, but not willing, to work at the jobs offered—no matter how ignominious—would not be eligible. 2) It provides a guarantee considerably *below* the level necessary to survive in a typical urban area. In essence, Nixon intends to replace the major parts of the War on Poverty programs with his welfare plan, plus revenue-sharing to the cities.

The latest chapter (February, 1972) in the Nixon welfare reform story reveals that the president will propose to Congress that the income maintenance program be started on a small, experimental scale, rather than through sweeping legislation. Apparently, this new plan is aimed at—among other things—assuaging the pique of the powerful Senator Ribicoff of Connecticut, who, because he was unhappy with Administration efforts in welfare reform, had indicated he would not lend his critical support to the Administration in getting its program through Congress.[26] Whatever the real story is here, it will probably be of little interest to the poor, whose lives go on

26. *New York Times*, February 4, 1972, p. 1.

while the King and his Court play games of political intrigue not unlike those played in the despotic French courts of the seventeenth century. One is tempted to suggest that, as a sure way of speeding up presidential and congressional efforts to get income to poor people, we should (literally) starve both branches of Congress until a vote providing an adequate income for poor people is forthcoming. At the very least, this would allow social scientists the opportunity to test the controversial issue of whether deprivation leads to an increase or a decrease in motivation.

HOUSING AND ANTISLUM LEGISLATION

Since the New Deal, and before, many reformers have been convinced that the principal cause of the persistence of poverty is, quite simply, the home or immediate surroundings of poor people. These reformers, therefore, have had at the heart of their antipoverty programs provision for "decent housing" for poor people. The first Federal public housing legislation in 1937 was clearly intended to provide housing for the *working* poor, thus giving them decent surroundings which would make them more inclined to continue participating in the labor market. Not surprisingly, housing provided by the 1937 legislation was, and still is, available only to those whose income is below some maximum level. What has happened is that many of the working poor have been forced to move to private housing as they got higher wages or better jobs. As a consequence, public housing has become increasingly occupied by the unemployed poor, especially welfare families and old people.

In any case, the public housing legislation of the 1930's was supplemented in 1949 by the urban renewal program. The purpose of this legislation was to provide more housing, but also to rehabilitate and redevelop slum areas by tearing down the old houses and business structures, and replacing them with clean, modern, government-subsidized housing and industry. The urban renewal program is in keeping with the liberal's fundamental assumption that changing the environment of the poor is as important as any other single measure in ending their poverty. A family on public assistance, the breadwinner of which is enrolled in a manpower training program, will be better off, it is argued, if it resides in a clean, safe neighborhood, and in a clean, safe house or apartment. One can hardly argue with this notion. The difference between the plan and what actually happened, however, is considerable, and we will discuss this difference shortly. These early programs were supplemented by legislation adopted during 1959–61 which subsidized homeownership for the low- to moderate-income family, the elderly, and the handicapped.[27]

Then came the War on Poverty in 1964 and additional legislation over the next four years. In this "war," full and explicit recognition was made of the existence of the "culture of poverty." The major programs in the effort, in addition to rent supplements and other housing subsidy programs, were Head Start, Neighborhood Youth Corps, VISTA (Volunteers in Service to America), Community Action programs, Model Cities programs, the Job Corps, additional educational funds to low-income neighborhoods, Neighborhood Legal Services, adult education, and all the rest. These programs were intended to supplement existing public assistance benefits and other antipoverty legislative measures, and to extend old programs like urban renewal and public housing. Among other goals, all were aimed at trying to stop the "cycle of poverty," whereby the children of the poor very quickly acquire the personal characteristics which have led their parents into poverty in the first place. (The ultimate implication of such a view, of course, is distilled in Edward Banfield's suggestion that poor children could be put in year-round boarding houses, or sold outright in a competitive market at the earliest possible age and brought up in circumstances more consistent with their later employability.)[28]

What was especially striking about the War on Poverty was the clear implication that the environment in which the poor lived was an important, if not the most important, cause of their

27. For a review of this legislation, see Robert Taggart, III, *Low Income Housing: A Critique of Federal Aid* (Baltimore: Johns Hopkins Press, 1970).

28. See Banfield, pp. 229–232.

poverty. This does not, as it may appear at first glance, amount to a contradiction of my earlier argument that the key feature of the liberal's theory is that poverty is caused by the personal characteristics of the poor. The liberal academic typically connects the personal characteristics of the poor with their *immediate* neighborhood environment. In the liberal view, therefore, the local environment is simply another "characteristic" of the poor which needs changing. Of course, one possible extension of the hypothesis that slums are inclined to nurture poverty is that the larger capitalist society is also inclined to nurture slums. This extension, however, could lead to the suggestion that poverty is *caused* by slums, which are an irrevocable result of industrial capitalism. Such an inference, of course, really means that capitalism *causes* poverty. That the liberal does not draw this inference is an important distinction between liberals and radicals, as they are defined herein, which leads them toward entirely different antipoverty policies. The liberal academic, wed to the assumption that poverty can be eliminated in our social order, *must* stop just this side of explaining slums as a consequence of that social order.

THE DEVELOPMENT OF BLACK NEIGHBORHOODS

Recently, a growing number of antislum policies have been suggested to deal specifically with the economic and social environments of black urban ghettos.[29] Some of the more moderate of these programs are familiar to most people, and the moderate ones are a logical outgrowth of the "culture of poverty" thesis. For example, "black capitalist" schemes are attempts to develop the economy of ghettos and to broaden the basis of political and economic control over black neighborhoods. The assumption of such schemes is generally that participation in black-owned and black-operated business firms will help teach underskilled blacks the rules and regulations of successful competition in labor markets and will instill in them a new pride in

29. An informative review of these kinds of programs, ranging from black capitalism to Muslim separatism, is in William Henderson and Larry Ledebur, *Economic Disparity: Problems and Strategies for Black America* (New York: Free Press, 1970).

whatever efforts they make. Similar programs, like Eugene Foley's "A Marshall Plan for the Ghetto," seek to increase by a huge amount the role of Federal financing in such programs, but the basic goal is the same.[30] Of course, the Reverend Jesse Jackson's Operation Breadbasket, with its emphasis on developing black business and on "buying black," and his more recent People United to Save Humanity (PUSH), both fit this model, as does the Reverend Leon Sullivan's Opportunity Industrialization Center in Philadelphia.

An extension of this model, though different in certain important aspects, is the Community Development Corporation, suggested in detail first by Roy Innis of CORE (Congress of Racial Equality).[31] Here the emphasis is on generating local funds for local investment projects, more broadly based than other "black capitalist" schemes, and the plan is to increase local control over the ghetto economy and to *share* whatever growth may occur in it.

The most important distinction which can be made between ghetto development schemes proposed by blacks and those proposed by white liberals concerns the final goal of such schemes. Blacks most frequently have advocated ghetto rebuilding because they believe the internal development of black ghettos is the only possible way to avoid assistance from whites and at the same time be geographically separated from whites. On the other hand, white liberals advocate ghetto rebuilding because, typically, they believe it to be an important part of any series of programs which will eventually provide for the dispersal of the ghetto into integrated suburbs. This means, of course, that more white ghetto rebuilders are integrationists than are blacks who advocate quite similar programs.

ANTIDISCRIMINATION LAWS

As everyone knows, there has been a great deal of public attention paid to civil rights legislation during the past decade. As

30. Eugene Foley, *The Achieving Ghetto* (Washington, D.C.: National Press, 1968).

31. As a start, see William Haddad and G. Douglas Pugh, eds., *Black Economic Development* (Englewood Cliffs: Prentice-Hall, 1969), especially Chapter 4, by Innis.

much as anything else, this has reflected the growing awareness of white Americans of the extent to which black poverty, and black problems generally speaking, are caused by white racism. Neither the extent of racism nor its precise relationship to black problems has been determined, nor will it ever be. Nonetheless, in these days only the most unenlightened continue to deny that racism plays an important role in keeping most blacks from participating on an equal basis in the economic and political life of the nation. Naturally, antidiscrimination proposals have become an integral part of liberal antipoverty efforts.

The laws and customs of this nation have surely reflected the growing popularity and power of this particular part of the liberal rhetoric. For example, a major civil rights act was passed in 1964, and the Voting Rights Act was passed in 1965. Both these acts sought to expand the rights of black Americans to work, live, play, and vote, and a special emphasis of the legislation was to place the full power of the Federal government at the disposal of blacks (or their attorneys) who felt that state or local governments had violated rights granted them by the Federal Constitution. In addition, there has been growing pressure on several Federal bureaucracies to encourage them to implement their programs so as to minimize segregation patterns in central cities. One prominent result of the new pressure, mentioned in the previous chapter, is that the Department of Housing and Urban Development has indicated its intention to deny funds for housing projects where the effect of such loans "will be to increase segregation patterns in central cities." In the past, Federal funds have been used by many local officials as a way to increase segregation by building low-income or public housing in undesirable, increasingly segregated neighborhoods.

In addition, recent Federal judicial interpretations of civil rights laws and of the Constitution have resulted in the busing of schoolchildren. Busing children in order to avoid segregated schools in urban areas assumes that there is a direct connection between the poverty of inner-city poor people and the relative inadequacy of their local schools, and thus falls neatly into the "culture of poverty" approach of the academic liberal. School-busing, of course, is considered antidiscriminatory activity, since

it is assumed that most of the students for whom better schooling will result are black children.

What can be said as a general summary of liberal antipoverty
programs is that they are thoroughly consistent with the basic
assumptions of the theory of poverty on which they are based. It
is important to note that exceedingly few of the programs reviewed here have generated a very serious threat to existing
power relationships at the various levels of government. (One
aspect of the War on Poverty, Community Action programs, did
clearly threaten local power groups in certain cities where Community Action agencies began to accumulate significant political power. Especially important was the program in Syracuse,
New York, under the tutelage of longtime community organizer
the late Saul Alinsky. However, as soon as it was clear that the
Federal legislation written in 1964 could actually be interpreted
as giving *real power* to poor people in local communities, the
legislation was revised, and in 1967 all Community Action agencies were more securely placed under the control of local politicians.[32])

What has happened to antipoverty efforts over the past decade, therefore, has actually been little more than a gradual expansion of their basic original provisions to accommodate the
"culture of poverty" thesis of academic social scientists and to
meet the clamor for "more action" on the part of increasingly
hostile and threatening slum-dwellers. As suggested earlier,
some people believe that the expansion of poverty programs in
the sixties was a response to urban riots more than to any other
single set of variables; that is, we take care of the urban poor
only *after* they threaten our own safety rather than working on
their problems because we have civilized values inconsistent
with their plight. This analysis may well be true, but it is also
the case that, once the decision was made to expand welfare
and antipoverty legislation, the character of the expanded pro-

32. An analysis of the agencies' faults and possibilities is the theme of
Kenneth Clark and Jeanette Hopkins, *A Relevant War Against Poverty*
(New York: Metropolitan Applied Research, 1968).

gram has followed remarkably closely the research findings of academic social scientists.

It is surely true that in this review of liberal policies none of the legislation which has been passed over the years to minimize urban poverty can be considered "unreasonable." Of course, the "reasonableness" of liberal reform should be expected since academic liberals, as well as congressional liberals, are the best imaginable witnesses to what "reasonableness" is all about. One won't be taken seriously in the Academy if one's latest plan for the future amounts to a serious challenge to the conventional wisdom on the matter, and one won't be re-elected, for example, if one's latest bill introduced in the Senate calls for a substantial shift in wealth and power among American citizens.

IV. An Appraisal of the Liberal Antipoverty Program

How well has the antipoverty program of the liberal reformers actually worked over the past thirty years or so, given its *own* goals? This is a terribly difficult question to answer, if one thinks about it for any time at all, since it implies a second question: what would the dimensions of urban poverty be had it *not* been for the reform measures aimed at eliminating it? What follows are some interesting, though by no means conclusive, data on some of the programs mentioned.

1. Regarding the success of cash supplement programs for low-income people, very few people doubt that these can be judged as anything other than a failure; indeed, a very little bit of information about them is all that is needed to support such an argument. Consider the following: [33]

a. In 1968, only one-third of those who were unemployed actually were receiving unemployment compensation, because of

33. Unless otherwise indicated, the data in this section come from the *Statistical Abstract of the United States: 1971*, and various 1970 Federal census publications.

gaps in the coverage and because of the expiration of benefits to those eligible. Moreover, in 1970, the average weekly unemployment payment was fifty dollars, about 37 percent of the average weekly wage in the nation. These payments are clearly not adequate to maintain the health, education, and welfare of their recipients. Of course, the inability to get unemployment compensation, because one either is ineligible or has used up one's benefits, shoves the unemployed into the welfare line with those who never got a job in the first place. Here the story is also dismal.

b. Because the states administer public assistance programs, the extent to which the poor receive welfare benefits depends largely on where they are located. (It will be recalled that, for example, AFDC and state welfare payments to a family of four ranged from $66 in Mississippi to $332 in Massachusetts in 1968.) Also, in this context, one should mention a subtle, though unmeasurable, aspect of how well the poor actually benefit from these programs. State and local welfare offices differ radically over the country in terms of how eager each is to administer its funds and what fundamental philosophy each has about poor people. Thus, the welfare agency in city A, even though provided with fewer state funds for its programs, may do a "better" job for its clients than the agency in city B, simply because the latter is directed or staffed by persons unsympathetic to the problems of the poor. If one will only think for a moment about how humiliating the welfare queue can be made by a hostile, contemptuous clerk, one can perhaps see how important is this dimension of any welfare program.

In addition to these limitations of public assistance programs, there is an even more serious one, which, surprisingly, has only recently been developed in published material. This limitation concerns the possibility that the primary purpose of welfare over the years has been *to guarantee a marginal work force at the bottom of the economic order.* Piven and Cloward sum up their detailed and persuasive argument on this matter by stating:

> Relief arrangements are ancillary to economic arrangements. Their chief function is to regulate labor, and they do that in two

general ways. First, when mass unemployment leads to outbreaks of turmoil, relief programs are ordinarily initiated or expanded to absorb and control enough of the unemployed to restore order; then, as turbulence subsides, the relief system contracts, expelling those who are needed to populate the labor market. . . . Some of the aged, the disabled, the insane, and others who are of no use as workers are left on the relief-rolls, and their treatment is so degrading and punitive as to instill in the laboring masses a fear of the fate that awaits them should they relax into beggary and pauperism. To demean and punish those who do not work is to exalt by contrast the meanest labor at the meanest rates. . . .[34]

One implication of this argument is that the liberal reformer has unwittingly joined hands with his conservative foes by establishing a welfare program which has no other real effect than to keep the poor—at the price of considerable humiliation to them—hanging on a limb, the *best* fruits of which are either low wage rates in marginal industries or even lower welfare rates. Their argument also explains the relatively low welfare payments in southern states. Since wages in the South are relatively low, it is necessary, in order to regulate the labor force, to keep welfare payments below local wages so that when jobs do appear, welfare recipients can be forced into them at wages higher than their welfare payments. Of course, the only tonic for these ills is a guaranteed annual income, nationally administered, which does not have a "work incentive" stipulation attached to it, and which is high enough to encourage people to ignore ignominious, low-paying jobs.

c. The Food Stamp and Surplus Food programs, which are meant to augment welfare benefits, are used by only *one-sixth* of those actually covered by the legislation (5.4 million of the 29 million who are eligible), chiefly because of a failure to implement the programs adequately at the state and local level, and a failure of bureaucrats to request funds or food even when their constituency includes many people eligible for them. In addition, the school lunch program, especially geared to provide for poor schoolchildren, presently covers only about half of those el-

34. Piven and Cloward, pp. 3–4.

igible. The reasons for this failure range from the fact that many school systems are too poor to support the program to the fact that school officials in some areas are unsympathetic to the program.[35]

d. The Medicare program, which covers old people, has been supplemented in most states by Medicaid, which covers low-income people. But in the case of Medicare, because of hostility to the program by state officials and doctors, or indifference to the problems of the poor, only about 35 percent of the total health bills of people over sixty-five years old has been paid in recent years.[36] In addition, the Medicaid program has been especially prone to extortion and fraud. Though no one knows how many doctors, pharmacists, and dentists have made themselves rich by treating poor people covered by Medicare and Medicaid, some revelations about how Medicaid has been working in New York City are revealing. An article in the *New York Times* (February, 1972) reported that ten of twelve defendants had pleaded guilty to a charge of stealing some two million dollars from the city's Medicaid program in recent years. Also, the *New York Times* reported that the city's only Medicaid office had advised that applicants for the program (all people on public assistance and many low-income people) line up *before dawn* in order to guarantee that their cases would be taken care of in the same day.[37] In essence, the whole enterprise was found to be a mess and a terrible distortion of its original intentions.

2. The results of programs to insure demand in the labor market is similar to those of public assistance. I have already

35. Sar Levitan, *Programs in Aid of the Poor for the 1970's* (Baltimore: Johns Hopkins Press, 1969), p. 97.

36. Fred Anderson, "The Growing Pains of Medical Care," *New Republic,* January 17, 1970. In order to rectify the medical service problem, at least that part which stems from a shortage of doctors and nurses, in November, 1971, the president signed the 1971 Comprehensive Health Manpower Training Act and the Nurse Training Act. These acts call for expenditures of about four billion dollars over the next three years, and the plan is to increase enrolments in medical schools by about twelve hundred students during 1972. The acts are also aimed at increasing the proportion of black doctors and nurses.

37. *New York Times*, November 29, 1971, p. 17.

pointed out that the Nixon anti-inflation program in the late 1960's and early 1970's was carried out disproportionately at the expense of the unemployed, especially those in the city, where unemployment is higher and more sensitive to changes in the level of income at the national level. In addition, there is increasing evidence that manpower training programs, and other similar programs aimed at increasing the "human capital" of poor people, are based upon some serious misconceptions about why people are poor.

This matter is worth some elaboration. Several researchers, especially Ivar Berg and Bennett Harrison, have done studies indicating that there is *not* a very strong relationship between education and productivity in many urban labor markets.[38] This surprising situation derives to an important degree from the fact that the credentials for many jobs are not consistent with the actual needs of the jobs themselves. For example, Berg has discovered that in several labor markets people with less than high school degrees are *more* productive than their fellow workers who have higher educational attainments. He explains this largely in terms of the higher transience of the more educated workers and the greater job commitment of the workers with less schooling. The point is that many workers are denied high wages because they lack credentials which are actually unnecessary in terms of the skill demanded by the job. It may be, as Berg suggests, that what many of the working poor need most is less "credentialism" in job markets, along with more years in school.

Other researchers have shown that many jobs in "marginal" industries do not pay adequate wages for full-time work, regardless of the personal characteristics of the workers (this is a point taken up earlier, in Chapter 2). The average full-time worker in many retail establishments, in nursing homes, and in hotels makes a wage which, on an annual basis, is below the govern-

38. See Ivar Berg, *Education and Jobs: The Great Training Robbery* (New York: Praeger, 1970); and Bennett Harrison, "Education and Underemployment in the Urban Ghetto," in David Gordon, ed., *Problems in Political Economy: An Urban Perspective* (Lexington, Mass.: Heath, 1970), pp. 181–190.

ment's absolute poverty level. Barry Bluestone describes the industries and the principal results of their "marginal" status as follows:

> Absolute productivity is well below that of all industry; less capital is utilized in production; profit rates are smaller; and most importantly, competition flourishes. The ability of many low-wage industries to pay adequate wages without drastically cutting employment is seriously open to question. Furthermore, the repressive environment decidedly stymies union organization and the pressure of unions for higher wages. Where an industry is so established that entry is free and open to new, unorganized firms, we can expect weak unions and most probably low wages. Where industries are marked by easy entry, fierce national and international competition, highly elastic product demand, low profits, and low productivity, we can almost be assured of two things: if a union exists at all, it is bound to be weak and ineffective, and there will surely be large numbers of working poor. . . .[39]

This evidence by Berg and Bluestone is in clear conflict with arguments that the more manpower training we receive the more likely we are to make a high salary, especially if we are poor to begin with.

3. Programs aimed at changing the environment in poor areas, such as slum redevelopment, urban renewal, Model Cities, Community Action, and the various housing laws, have met similar bleak fates in the real world. Consider the following data:

a. While there are currently 7 million people eligible for public housing, only 700,000 units have been built since 1937. A good part of the reason for this lies in the unwillingness of local governments to ask for funds that are available from the Federal government because of the local citizenry's hostility to public housing programs. In addition, when these projects have been designed, they have been so ill-financed that the typical housing

39. Barry Bluestone, "The Characteristics of Marginal Industries," in Gordon, p. 106.

project is a catastrophe: [40] it is usually located in a slum, seems to be designed to approximate a penal institution, and is *typically* directed by a middle-class, white male who is hostile to the people in his project and thoroughly ignorant about the dimension or character of their problems.[41] Since the majority of the people now living in projects are either poor, black, female, or all three, there has emerged a growing unwillingness on the part of suburbanites to allow low-income housing projects in their neighborhoods, and this has become the most considerable barrier to the success of such programs.[42] More recent housing legislation has failed to have much impact, in terms of the number of houses actually built for poor people, again because the typical program is underfinanced, because of fraudulent practices by public officials or private citizens who carry out the programs, or because of the hostility to such programs by the middle class in cities which most need this housing.

b. The idea that urban renewal has had harsh effects on poor people is not terribly controversial. Between 1949 and 1961, for example, while 126,000 low-income houses were destroyed by urban renewal, only 28,000 new housing units were provided,[43] and this trend has continued. Between 1949 and 1966, of the forty-two thousand acres cleared for renewal projects, only twenty thousand of these were destined for residential use. The original legislation provided for relocation funds for households being replaced by slum clearance, but since 1949 less than 0.5 percent of the total urban renewal budget has actually been used to relocate families. Moreover, because of the general shortage of low-income housing in this country, families replaced and relocated have been forced to move from their neighborhoods, with

40. See especially Lee Rainwater, *Behind Ghetto Walls: Black Families in a Federal Slum* (Chicago: Aldine, 1970).

41. On this point, see Charles Hartman and Greg Carr, "Housing the Poor," *Trans-Action*, December, 1969, pp. 49–53.

42. For example, see Linda and Paul Davidoff and Neil Gold, "The Suburbs Have to Open Their Gates," *New York Times Magazine*, November 7, 1971, pp. 40–60.

43. Cited in Herbert Gans "The Failure of Urban Renewal: A Critique and Some Plans," in Louis K. Loewenstein, ed., *Urban Studies* (New York: Free Press, 1971), p. 368.

all the attendant disorganization of their lives, into even costlier housing. In Chicago, for example, families replaced by urban renewal moved from demolished homes which, on the average, cost them 35 percent of their income to houses which cost them 46 percent of their income. Also, a study by Chester Hartman showed that the median rents of Boston West Enders (who were relocated by urban renewal) increased from forty-one to seventy-one dollars.[44]

Some critics of urban renewal programs, in trying to explain their failure, argue that urban renewal has been sidetracked from its original purpose of helping poor slum-dwellers and has become, in the typical project, a boondoggle for business firms.[45] Since the Federal government picks up a good part of the tab for renewal projects, what has happened quite frequently is that the demolished slums have been replaced by luxury housing, by business firms not serving the relocated poor, or by cultural centers. In trying to grasp the essentials of the liberal imagination, it might be instructive here to consider what might have been done for poor people in Washington, D.C., had the funds spent on the Kennedy Center for the Performing Arts been spent instead on low-income housing. The Center, conceived and financed by upper-class liberals, is an especially good example of the kind of misuse of funds which leads radicals to doubt that liberals can be trusted to solve the problems of poor people. After all, one might ask, how many liberals do you know *personally* who would advocate, for example, destroying the Metropolitan Opera House in New York City, which is primarily patronized by upper- and middle-class people, and replacing it with an amusement park and movie theaters which would cater to the recreational needs of poor people (of whom there are fewer and fewer because Lincoln Center has attracted more and more "beautiful people" to the area, forcing up rents and driving out poor people). It is an interesting question to ponder.

In any case, the result of many redevelopment programs is to push the original inhabitants of the demolished houses into an

44. *Ibid*.
45. For example, Danny Beagle, Al Haber, and David Wellman, "Creative Capitalism and Urban Redevelopment," in Gordon, pp. 400–404.

already crowded low-income housing market, and, not surprisingly, a disproportionate number are black. As rather substantial support of James Baldwin's claim that "urban renewal is Negro Removal," consider a study of the controversial renewal project in Hamtramck, Michigan, a suburb of Detroit. This study showed that 70 percent of the twelve hundred people replaced by one renewal project in that city (an urban highway built through a predominately black neighborhood) were black, and that *none* of them were given the relocation funds provided by urban renewal legislation. The overall racial effect of Hamtramck urban renewal programs from 1960 to 1966 was to reduce the black population in the city from 14.5 percent to 8.5 percent. At this point, the project has been stalled by a judicial order based upon the claim of certain blacks in the area that their removal was a chief goal of the whole redevelopment scheme.[46]

4. The "black redevelopment" programs have yet to either catch the imagination of many blacks or dip into the budgets of important governments. It is probably too early to evaluate with much authority the effects on the ghetto of schemes like Operation Breadbasket, Community Development Corporations, or "Marshall Plans." To the extent, however, that they share with liberal reform models the assumption that it is possible to develop the ghetto economy by a heavy dependence on funds from white governments and the great American industrial firms, they may be destined for the failure that has befallen most liberal reform programs.

5. Finally, the spate of antidiscrimination laws passed over the years have, to put it mildly, fallen enormously short of their intended goals. The 1970 Civil Rights Commission report suggested that because of inadequate funding and staffing, and because of the unsympathetic views of many civil rights officials, the civil rights laws of this nation are not being enforced. In the dry language of the report, there is a "gap between civil rights guarantees and what has actually been delivered." [47]

46. *New York Times*, November 24, 1971, p. 19.

47. From the statement of its chairman, the Reverend Theodore Hesburgh, *New York Times*, October 13, 1970, p. 28.

What, then, finally can be made of all this? What has been the record of liberal reformist attempts to eliminate urban poverty? On the basis of this brief review of the most important reformist programs, one could conclude that they simply don't work, and this conclusion would not be inconsistent either with the statistical facts on the matter, to the extent that they have been gathered, or with any number of available critical appraisals. Even granting that the programs have failed, there are still at least two inferences about the causes of failure that could be drawn from the data.

First, one could argue that the programs' failure derives from the general incompatability of most such programs with the world view of the state and local bureaucracies that implemented them. Such explanations are generally seized upon by liberal reformists, who never let the failure of pet programs corrode their belief that reform of the system is both possible and desirable. Moreover, additional financing is possible, as is a change in the consciousness of local bureaucrats. Obviously, given such a view, the need is for ever-greater dedication to reform politics and polemics. A recent popular version of this view goes like this: If we could only convince a majority of Americans that human welfare is more important than fighting socialism every time it appears in some remote jungle, we could re-allocate the defense budget and solve all our problems. This, of course, is the "priority" explanation given by most liberals. There is probably much merit to the argument, and I suspect almost everyone is aware of its basic ingredients.

Of course, a second inference one might draw from the failure of liberal reform to significantly change the conditions of the poor is a potentially more damaging one (and one which would have been predicted by the radical analyst all along). We have reviewed the basic features of the radical paradigm earlier, and it will be remembered that in the radical model, for various and sundry reasons, liberal reform is held to be a logical impossibility. Radicals assume that it must fail, and when it does, it's no surprise. It is, as a matter of fact, precisely the failure of reform politics that helped create the growing radical movement in the 1960's and is at the basis of most of the radical analyses currently being made.

So—where do you go, if you conclude that liberal reform is a blind alley? Back to the drawing board? Into a monastery, to wait it out? The following chapter attempts to answer this question, or at least to present a better way of thinking about it.

Chapter Five

ON REVOLUTIONARY POLITICS

A Short Political Autobiography

In trying to determine what I might pick to include in this chapter from all the millions of words written on radicalism, revolution, and poverty, I have asked myself several questions: Should I concentrate on *socialism* in general, since most radical antipoverty policies are fundamentally collectivist? Should I concentrate on revolutionaries, or on radicals who are not trying to overthrow the system? Or should I review the latest antipoverty programs which, in terms of either the ends of the programs or the means proposed to achieve these ends, could be classified as radical?

Finally, I decided against such a review and instead chose to explain in some detail my own personal movement from one camp to the other—from liberalism to radicalism, to fantasies about revolution, to despair, to liberalism, and so on—during the past decade. I believe this personal history may be of some interest; I hope so. It may also be of some value in understanding the current debate between revolutionaries, radical academics, and liberal reformists about how best to obliterate the misery in the city that all consider intolerable.[1]

Of course, personal histories ordinarily appear in autobiographies, novels which closely parallel the author's life, or travelogues, and I recognize that my own experience may seem especially obtrusive as a final chapter to this book. Given our commitment in modern times to a belief in the distinction between scientific facts and "other information," it will appear to many readers, perhaps, that I have transcended the legitimate boundaries of a book such as this one. To my mind, however, the distinction between different kinds of facts is blurred, especially when these facts are comments on human behavior, and I trust the argument in Chapter 3 provided some reasons why I deny this distinction.[2] After all, the best guide to life in pre-classical Greece is Homer, a *blind*, lyrical poet; and can one find a more vivid, informative account of life in nineteenth-century London than in Dickens's novels, or a truer account of the tragedy of the Spanish civil war than Hemingway's *For Whom the Bell Tolls*, or a more believable version of the life and times of Elizabethan royalty than that given in Shakespeare's plays? Is the statement "We are such stuff as dreams are made of" a less valid one than the observation that "over one-third of the American people live in urban areas"? I don't think so. Each has its own particular form and substance, but each transmits a different message to all the different human souls who hear

1. In what follows, I have drifted somewhat from the principal theme of "solving urban poverty." Here I shall discuss my political response to a decade or so of being committed to socialism as the organizing principle of American society. Being a socialist is, for most of us socialists, anyway, basically defined as being opposed to the mass poverty and grossly inequitable income distribution which, at one time or the other, characterizes all industrial capitalist societies. Therefore, my experience since about 1960 in trying to build socialism has also been the experience of trying to minimize urban poverty.

2. Needless to say, these views about the dichotomy between factual and nonfactual statements are certainly not unique, though, alas, many social scientists would consider them slightly odd and idiosyncratic. For an especially informative discussion of this particular part of the debate on methodology, see Steven Toumin, *Foresight and Understanding: An Inquiry into the Aims of Science* (New York: Harper & Row, 1963).

it and reinterpret it in terms of their own unique histories.

There are aspects of our existence which simply do not lend themselves to objective observation in the scientific sense of that term, and political behavior seems an especially good example. Norman Mailer's essay on the 1968 political conventions, *Miami and the Siege of Chicago*,[3] excellently demonstrates the superiority of the novelist-journalist in describing how our political system actually functions. My approach in this chapter is, therefore, the result of a decision to use what I consider the most appropriate method, given the nature of the material of this chapter and given my political experience; and I believe that what follows does as much to add to our understanding of the problem and its solution as any of the other "facts" which are found in these pages.

I. A Personal Note on Revolutionary Politics

To begin with, I have thought of myself as a socialist since those wistful days when an old professor at Texas University, Robert Montgomery, convinced me finally that the institutions of capitalism were on balance a considerable detriment to the human situation. By remembering his own experience as a young rebel, then as a socialist, then as a prominent New Dealer, Dr. Montgomery captured my imagination as did no other teacher with visions of delightful alternatives to the present order of things. This experience was around 1959, during the last stages of the Eisenhower years, a period which I felt at the time must surely have been the most pathetic of this country's history. I sensed very strongly during those years that this nation's preoccupation with communism, its ethnocentric need to be best in everything, would finally result in one, or perhaps more than one, ghastly catastrophe: racial war; world war; dreadful economic stagnation; military domination; or, along with the Soviet Union, a final brutal submission of every little country in the world.

Dr. Montgomery's model of a different order of things, sup-

3. Norman Mailer, *Miami and the Siege of Chicago* (New York: Signet, 1968).

ported by the images of some other teachers and many fellow students, led me toward a whole decade of confusion about how best to "build socialism," the only alternative I could imagine which might solve poverty, end wars, and, in general, save us all. This judgment that the marvelous promises of capitalism were fraudulent was given considerable impetus by my enrollment in graduate school in 1961, an act determined as much as anything by my not being able to find a job I wanted after finishing my undergraduate work as an economics major. By that time, I had three children, and the prospect of working in Washington for the Labor Department for fifty-four hundred dollars or being a department manager trainee for a department store in Houston—my two offers—were too dismal to face. Thus, I took the Graduate Record Exams, barely passed them, and began graduate courses. My initial aim was to study for a master's degree, thus fending off employment for a year or so and also getting some time to work through my new hostility towards all those jobs in the capitalist system in which I no longer believed.

Graduate school provided me with a greater variety of experiences than I had ever imagined and, at times, almost more than I could cope with psychologically. Primarily through small subsidies from the economics department and a very large subsidy from my wife's employment, I was able to spend the better part of the next five years (1961–65) doing little more than study the American economy, that monster which to my mind was destroying us all. Graduate school provided me with the opportunity to clear my thoughts about capitalism, though for the first three years I must admit to less clarity and a great deal more of using my studies to augment my argument that socialism must be developed to replace the decadent capitalist system. I found in each course, no matter what its substance or how it was taught, some tidbit which provided colorful new evidence to support my very subjective evaluation of the two systems.

Indeed, I was the most outgoing socialist of all; at least, as I try to remember it now, I was one of the strongest and most vociferous advocates of the end of capitalism and the triumphant emergence of socialism. No argument about the alleged merits of capitalism or the inherent problems of socialism could budge me from my rock of righteousness. I simply would not move. I have frequently looked back on these years with some nostalgia, for with the exception of my youth, when I had no particular views about anything (other than sex and athletics), I have never been so sure of my understanding of things. Socialism, at least my own brand, seemed so obviously a superior way to do things. Why couldn't everyone see this? Also, as I look back on these years, I can hardly remember the detailed dimensions of what was most wrong with capitalism and what kind of socialism I had in mind as a substitute. Probably my explantion went something like this: there is a lot of poverty and greed in the United States. Also, America has a history of wars, none of which can easily be separated totally from the need of capitalism for foreign markets, nor the necessity for the human fodder of capitalism to live a competitive, aggressive personal life style. The drive to compete at home became the foundation for trying to force the submission of those abroad who seemed inclined in another direction. And, given the preoccupation in this country with communism, I felt strongly that American capitalism contained the roots of world ruin.

From this world view, I reasoned that the salvation of Americans, at least, depended upon getting free from the dreadful, deadly institutions of capitalism and replacing them with more cooperative habits. A cooperative spirit, I thought, would solve the problem of poverty and deprivation at home, and given a new world view, we would all see the error of our ways and gradually learn to love, or at least hate less, those societies that were trying in their own ways to solve problems collectively. In other words, we needed socialism.

Now, as everyone knows, there are myriad varieties of "socialism," ranging from totalitarian central planning in the Soviet Union to the democratic welfare-socialism of the Scandinavian states. In between are the experiences of Yugoslavia, with its "workers' socialism," Britain's "welfare state," and an endless variety of alternatives, mainly in the young, independent nations in Asia, Africa, and Latin America. I had to choose from these, and I knew at the time that my choice would necessarily be based on a second great faith—faith in some brand of "democracy;" that is, my kind of socialism would have to be the result of the aspirations of *most* Americans. I was not then, nor am I now, inclined toward palace coups, replete with dashing soldiers and new economic plans. I was, therefore, drawn toward the Scandinavian model, especially the one in Sweden. Like so many others on the left, I fancied Sweden a nation whose life was based on sane compromise, impervious to the twisted rhetoric of America and the Soviet Union, a nation which had embarked upon its own transition to a more cooperative and just social order.

However, I very definitely viewed the Swedish welfare state as a transitional step toward true socialism, thinking that the experience of partial cooperation would demonstrate to the Swedes how little could be gained from *any* competition. I thus assumed that in the not too distant future the Swedes, or some similar society, would pass into that wonderful state I dreamed of as "democratic socialism," where everyone was "given to according to need and gave according to talent," and where the whole thing was unaminously voted in every four years or so! It was rather pleasant in those days to bask in the sun of my own righteousness. I had it all figured out; it was simply a matter of time and training before most everyone else would see the true path and follow prescient, budding intellectuals like myself.

Given this view of what kind of social order was necessary, and given my taste for "democracy," I necessarily eschewed the pleas of the militant revolutionaries, whose models insisted upon the violent upheaval of social institutions. I simply never had the taste for throwing bombs. Though certain about the need for an end to capitalism, I felt equally certain about the horror of violent revolutionary change. It did not occur to me until much later that there may be a nasty inconsistency in these two positions. It took the later 1960's to show me how very painful this contradiction can be to a simple soul trying to do what's "right."

I suppose that, deep down, I shared the point of view expressed in a conversation between Alyosha and Ivan in Dostoevsky's *The Brothers Karamazov* [4] (a story I came to know

4. Translation by Princess Alexandra Kropotkin (Garden City: Literary Guild of America, 1949), Part 2, Book 5, Chapter 4.

from conversations with my friend Jimmy Cooney). In a discussion about rebellion, Ivan confronts his brother with the following question:

> Tell me yourself, I challenge you—answer. Imagine that you are creating a fabric of human destiny with the object of making men happy in the end, giving them peace and rest at last, but that it was essential and inevitable to torture to death only one tiny creature—a baby beating its breast with its fist, for instance —and to found that edifice on its unavenged tears, would you consent to be the architect on those conditions? Tell me, and tell the truth.

When his brother answers, "No, I wouldn't consent," Ivan asks a second question: "And can you admit the idea that men for whom you are building it would agree to accept their happiness on the foundation of the unexpiated blood of a little victim? And accepting it would remain happy forever?" Again, Alyosha answers, "No!"

I am quite sure that there has been no time in my life when I could have answered "yes" to either of these two questions. And, during the early years of 1960, the reign of death and terror which I *knew* would accompany social upheaval always posed itself to me as an absolute argument against such an upheaval in the United States. No matter how badly deprived were the poor children in our many filthy, ugly, central-city slums, I believed they were better off than they would be with guerrilla warfare raging around their bedsides. Of course, on many occasions, such as the bombing of four young black children in an Alabama church, the assassination of Martin Luther King, the attacks on the Freedom Riders, the lunch counter sit-ins, the Selma marchers, the murder of the Chicago Black Panthers, the bombing raids in North Vietnam, My Lai, and all the other evidences of pathological violence emanating from American society, it has been exceedingly difficult for me to maintain a nonviolent stance.

Apparently, I never doubted for a long enough time to take revolutionary action that using violence to solve American social problems was shortsighted and probably damaging to the cause in the name of which it was carried out; in addition, I know that such action has always involved the random suffering of some people, including many for whom the revolution is being waged. Nevertheless, in some societies—China in the twentieth century is an excellent example—the argument for armed revolt must have seemed most compelling. China had been all but dismembered in the nineteenth century by Western imperialism, and had been directly threatened in the twentieth century by Japanese imperialism. For several centuries the Chinese had considered their land the "central kingdom," but by modern times China had been reduced to a decaying social order in which those people not starving in the countryside were being tyrannized in the city by colonialists from any number of Western countries. Chaos, or something similar, reigned in many parts of China, and to the revolutionary mind of both Chiang Kai-shek (with his Koumintang) and Mao Tse-tung (with his Red Army) the need for a pitched battle to wrest power from the established order must have seemed too obvious for serious debate.

I am aware of these kinds of situations, in which the desperation of the situation seems to compel one to take up arms. The nineteenth- and twentieth-century Chinese experience has, no doubt, been duplicated throughout all of human history. Indeed, I am aware that many contemporary societies are afflicted with totalitarian regimes in which the oppressors cannot be expected, by the wildest stretch of the imagination, to voluntarily relieve the agony of their victims (victims such as blacks in South Africa and Rhodesia; the Vietnamese, Laotians, and Thais; Russian Jews and intellectuals; the poor in Latin American dictatorships; antifascist Greeks and Spaniards—the list is endless). I do not know how best to present a pacifist's argument concerning these social orders, and I shall not even begin an attempt. But I will argue—and this is my essential point here—that these societies and the problems they face are fundamentally different, in many crucial respects, from the social order of the United States. Therefore, it does not necessarily follow that violent resistance, which one might consider justifiable in South Africa, is also justifiable (or reasonable) in the U.S.

First, in the United States, most people, indeed a great majority, are adequately provided for, in their own terms; at least they are provided for to the extent that they do not think of themselves as potential revolutionaries. Unlike South Africa, for example, where the oppressed are a clear and huge majority, most Americans receive enough from the social system to keep them in one of two quite moderate political parties. Second, social change through the political system is at least conceivable in America, though one might argue quite correctly that the difference between the oligarchy in the Soviet Union and that in the United States is one of degree. But the degree to which the two political systems differ is probably a crucial one.

Third, there has been, especially in the past three decades, a clear trend in America toward increased consideration for those who don't survive the competitiveness of the economy. We are slowly but surely becoming more acutely aware, as a people, of the large-scale deprivation among us, and our *ability* to do something about it markedly distinguishes us from most other nations in the world. Finally, we are so much more wealthy, so much more powerful, so much more efficient than other peoples that no fruitful comparisons can probably be made between our problems and the problems of others, and between possible ways to solve them. Indeed, the pace of social change in America makes us unique, even in terms of our own very immediate past.

To summarize: in my judgment, violent upheaval in this nation is neither possible nor desirable. It is not possible because the great majority of the people in the United States oppose it, and this majority includes the police, the military, the politicians, the working class, the middle class, the professors, the capitalists, and, probably, most of the poor, in whose name it would be staged. It is, therefore, not desirable because, among other reasons, it would be, finally, nothing more than a short-run aberration bound for quick defeat, but especially painful to many helpless people who cannot protect themselves from its deadly fallout. It would probably also usher in a kind of fascism for everyone to the left of the Democratic party.

Revolutions, generally speaking, are not fought in the backyards of the rich, for the rich are able to flee when the signs are ominous. The pitched battle by American guerillas will be fought downtown, as has clearly been the case in U.S. urban conflicts already, and the refugees on the streets and the back roads will most assuredly not be anyone other than the refugees in all such conflicts: the poor, the old, the weak, the defenseless. Behind the policemen, just on the other side of the late J. Edgar Hoover, crouching solidly and *en masse* behind the White House, have been *most* of the American people. At the present time they don't *want* a revolution, and it is precisely their lack of enthusiasm for anything other than moderate political change that makes the Nixons and McGoverns of this nation possible. In a word, those who fantasize about overthrowing the social order only fool themselves and their friends; the cop-killer and the bomb-thrower only cause the screws to be tightened further on everyone and everything to the left of the American center.

I realize, of course, that given my taste for socialism, and given my taste for nonviolent political change, I am left, if I want to engage in *conventional* political activity, with liberal reform. I should like to discuss that syndrome once again in the context of the past few remarks.

II. Another Look at Liberal Reform

Critics of liberal reform programs, of course, especially on the left, never cease to point out how often these programs don't work, frequently using the data presented in the previous chapter. I know about this criticism for I have, during the past ten years or so, been responsible for a good deal more than the average share of it. Throughout the 1960's a significant part of the rhetoric from the left has been righteous condemnation of liberal reform. The liberal has been held in contempt by a host of radicals: black and white panthers, student revolutionaries, and hippies on the left, and most everyone on the right. The liberal's advocacy of gradualism has been interpreted as counterrevolutionary by the left and "bleeding-heart socialism" by the right.

I shared in this criticism for a good part of the decade. And rather than face up to the contradiction in my own thinking regarding the choice between liberal reform and political upheaval, I sat on the sidelines, criticizing both. It was fun, until I let myself think about it more honestly. Doing so changed my mind quite significantly. It now seems clear to me that if one rejects the revolutionary models of the militant left, yet shares the liberal view that something must be done *in the short run* to minimize the disastrous fallout of a competitive social order, one has no other choice than to engage in reform politics in the conventional American way. Though my earlier discussion indicates how uneasy I feel with this conclusion, a few additional remarks about my politics over the past ten years should demonstrate why I accept this conclusion, however unenthusiastically.

I became "politicized," as they say, in 1960 by embracing the apparently liberal candidacy of John Kennedy. To me, as to so many moderate leftists at the time, Kennedy seemed to represent a breath of fresh air which would deliver us from what I considered the hatefulness of laissez-faire Republicanism. Indeed, even as late as 1964, my faith in liberals from the Democratic party had not abated, and it still seemed possible that Lyndon Johnson, the Texas populist, would be able to usher in the welfare state that we liberals had for so long thought necessary. The gradual disillusionment with these political heroes which followed from those early years of the 1960's is understandable to anyone who has kept his or her eyes open, even halfway. What made all the clay feet crumble was the Vietnam war.

The Vietnam war seemed to me, as it did to so many others on the left, overwhelming evidence that the American social order had become a monster. If the war didn't convince us, the riots in Watts, Detroit, and Newark did, and many of us settled swiftly into a more revolutionary frame of mind. The combination of brutal suppression of blacks and others at home, plus the unbelievable barbarity of the Vietnam war, so obviously a sham, so obviously based on the political needs of so few men, so catastrophic to this nation's self-esteem, drove me into a dark despair about my country. Since I was a college teacher throughout those years, I was reminded daily of the enormous toll that the war, the riots, and the general confusion were having on young people. How alien they felt themselves amidst the bleakness of it all. Then came 1968.

If, by 1968, one hadn't seen through the complex web of lies and distortions with which the Democratic Party attempted to cover up its handling of the war, the convention in Chicago that year surely must have cleared the air. I remember watching the convention in Ithaca, New York, with family and friends and weeping openly while the Chicago policemen beat mercilessly everyone and everything in sight. This must have been the lowest point of all, watching Hubert Humphrey and Edmund Muskie from the protection of the vast armory speak meaningless platitudes while a new kind of fascism marched madly just outside the hall. It was at that point that, for many of us, political upheaval seemed so obviously the only way out, the only potentially fruitful path to follow. After all, the Democratic party had for over thirty years been the cocoon in which liberal academics and the liberal element of the corporate world had done their particular thing. Humphrey, who watched his own nomination speeches while young people were being beaten and gassed outside his hotel window, had been the most outspoken liberal of them all! That night in August, 1968, was terrible for a lot of us, even those who were protected from the Chicago police by eight hundred miles of superhighways.

It was at this point in my life that the rhetoric of the revolutionary seemed most compelling. I read Eldridge Cleaver, Herbert Marcuse, Tom Hayden, and many others, and their arguments made sense, especially their condemnation of the kind of social order which allowed political hacks to speak for justice and freedom while participating in and supporting war and suppression anywhere it seemed politically advantageous. Thus, during 1969–70, my thinking, like that of so many others, was dominated more by fantasies about how to undo or overthrow the capitalist order (that is, a concentration on revolutionary means rather than ends) than by alternatives to that order. Get rid of the goddamn thing; what comes after it cannot possibly be worse!

I don't remember exactly when I began to move away from the model of the violent revolutionary and back to my "early" 1960's period, though I remember distinctly being threatened to the core every time I heard a black radical warn me of the necessity of my eventual demise, or sat and listened to the confused fantasies of white student revolutionaries. I distinctly recall being aware of the sad reality that I could think of no one on the radical left, not one, whom I would trust with control of that political order. I was drawn to the Black Panthers in their understandable militancy and enjoyed more than once the antics of the hippies; indeed, when Abbie Hoffman and his Yippie friends tossed dollar bills from the balcony of the stock market to the money people below, it represented to me the quintessence of guerilla theater. But, in spite of my sympathy for them and understanding of their needs, I could never rest comfortably with the image of Eldridge Cleaver as president, or Jerry Rubin as secretary of state. Not that Rubin would be worse than Dean Rusk—that seems virtually impossible—but he would not be a very great improvement.

So, by about 1970, I had come back to a position in many respects not too different from the one I had held in 1960. Though I was considerably less enthusiastic about liberal reform in 1970 than I had been in earlier years, this approach once again seemed at least a *feasible* alternative to the militant strategies that dominated the news in the 1960's. And I became, at the beginning of a new decade, more willing to consider the possibility that many liberals had reached their position only *after* having rejected violent political change for many of the same reasons I have done so. Thus, I now would argue that *within the framework of conventional politics*, there probably is no better way to minimize those problems associated with poverty, pollution, the transportation system, or the bizarre American health care system.

It must be emphasized here that I am not equating a thoroughly reformed American capitalism with socialism. My argument is only that such a reform is a necessary palliative, a necessary though not sufficient condition, for building socialism, whatever form that development might take. In other words, as we build toward an egalitarian social order, it will be easier knowing that the pain and suffering of the present system's losers are, to some extent, mitigated. Moreover, welfare capitalism has the very real effect of taking from violent revolutionaries the necessary social unrest for the success of their fantasized coups. I expect that most poor people, if given the choice, would prefer an inadequate guaranteed income and a crowded community health clinic to firebombs in the yard and rifle shots overhead. Briefly, the following is what I believe would be the basis of a liberal antipoverty program which would be consistent with the liberal's claim to have a genuine concern for the American poor.

III. Two Basic Elements of a Workable Liberal Antipoverty Program

BLACK ECONOMIC DEVELOPMENT

The comments in the previous section about liberal reform will seem outrageous to many, but perhaps especially so to those who are convinced that the welfare state is not a solution to the problems of American blacks. I am very much aware of all the arguments about the special case of American blacks, and, in fact, I argued explicitly in Chapter 3 that liberal reform as it has been conceived and implemented in the past will not solve the problems of black Americans. I do believe, though, as my argument in the previous section makes clear, that there is no political solution to their problems *in the near future.*

Many writers, black and white, have argued correctly that a real solution to black problems in the country would, at a minimum, depend upon control by blacks of their own neighborhoods, businesses, labor markets, etc. And other writers add that even with control of their own areas, in order to share in the wealth of this nation's economy, blacks would of necessity substitute more lucrative industries for the marginal, low-profit ones which most frequently are located in poor neighborhoods. In this scenario, where blacks have some control, but control over a poor part of the city, it is clear that any change which occurs will be slow indeed, even if the welfare state is in full operation. There is simply no way, in one fell swoop, that white Americans are going to make restitution for their historical deprivation of blacks. Indeed, the fact that *most* of the poor in the United States are white indicates that Americans will not quickly come to the aid of *anyone* who is down and out; this is one of those quaint customs of which many Americans are most proud.

My point is that blacks who fantasize about a change in the conscience of white Americans and a "Marshall Plan" for black ghettos in the near future are probably only fooling themselves. Many Americans hate the poor, and many more especially hate minority poor. As a consequence, the welfare state promises a little help for everyone, but not a lot for anyone, and, therefore, those currently on the bottom will continue to be there for some time.

Of course, many readers will respond to this last comment by agreeing and then asking: knowing this, why do you romanticize the welfare state; why not admit that the only hope for the black poor is violent revolution? It's difficult for me to answer this criticism, except to conjure up once more the deromanticized version of urban guerilla warfare, and to answer my critic by reminding him or her that the battles will be fought not in the suburbs but downtown. As the riots in black central cities have shown over and over and over again, the principal human victims are poor blacks or lower-middle-class white policemen. Urban guerilla warfare will simply not move to Grosse Pointe, Chicago's North Shore, or Westchester County. Moreover, most black people don't want violent revolution, as *every* national poll of black people ever conducted has clearly shown. In fact, most such polls indicate that blacks share with whites the view that increasing participation in the fat, sleek American economy represents the most desirable vehicle to a comfortable life. Black or white revolutionaries who would substitute their own dreams of violent usurpation of the establishment's power may be, therefore, no less tyrannical toward their own people than rednecks who waste themselves in a life of trying to keep the rest of the underclass below them.

To me, then, the special short-term problems of American blacks, if they are to be ameliorated at all, will be minimized best by some combination of welfare reform, "consciousness-raising" kinds of educational programs, local cooperation, and patience. I am also convinced that those models of black development which emphasize the *collective, internal* development of the slum's economic and political order probably have the best long-term prospects. Depending on whites for development funds in addition to welfare cash flows is probably to make a strategic error. I suppose my conclusion here is the rather unexciting one that of all the proposals for ghetto development, the economic plan of CORE, which emphasizes economic control through community development corporations, and the political efforts to control Newark, are examples of those with most promise for the long run.[5] There are, for better or for worse, simply no other kinds of paths to take in the short run, regardless of the insistence of the very small minority of blacks who champion a quicker way to wealth and power. Viewing the ghetto as a "colony" largely incapable of changing the larger society which surrounds it is probably the best basic framework in terms of which to imagine solutions to black urban poverty.

THE GUARANTEED ANNUAL INCOME

I think especially that the core of a liberal antipoverty program *must* be a guaranteed annual income at least high enough to provide an "adequate" minimum income to those who receive it.[6] (Perhaps the minimum income demanded by the National Welfare Rights Organization is a good guide to what is "adequate," at least from the viewpoint of those who will actually try to live on it. This figure was between six and seven thousand dollars in the early 1970's, and was rising.) I also advocate a guaranteed income *without* a work incentive, mainly because I am convinced that the typical poor person in this society has been economically disenfranchised; that is, the poor clearly are the victims of the long-term modernization of our economy, es-

5. See the section "The Economic Development of Black Neighborhoods" in the Bibliography for numerous discussions of various kinds of developmental plans.
6. For a review of the various programs, see David Gordon, ed., *Problems in Political Economy: An Urban Perspective* (Lexington, Mass.: Heath, 1970), pp. 249–254.

pecially in the agricultural sector. I can see no moral justification for forcing poor people into degrading jobs in order to satisfy our lust for the principle that whoever gets income must work for it (or be ready to work as soon as some marginal job becomes available). The American poor are the latest victims of the technological revolution. While the rest of us enjoy the fruits of technology because we were born in the right place at the right time, the poor sit on the sidelines, literally excluded from what the rest of us and the world think of as the "American economic order."

Of course, critics of a guaranteed income without a work incentive never cease to shriek about the horrid effects of such a plan on the labor market. It is alleged by many such critics, probably correctly, that if we institute a minimum guarantee of, say, four thousand dollars for an urban family of four, those who work full time for more—say forty-three hundred—will be inclined to quit and go on welfare. Maybe so. However, those in this society who work for forty-three hundred dollars a year are invariably employed in marginal industries in which the relatively low wage rate is accompanied by bad working conditions, relatively little job status, and relatively hard physical work or extremely tedious work. Why not free our working class from these kinds of jobs? Liberals and others have spent no little time over the years in rationalizing such American excesses as the terribly unequal distribution of wealth and income and the cold war, and no doubt they can also figure out economic, political, and historical justifications for ways to keep the economy functioning even though the least skilled fifth of the labor force is not *forced* to work.

In essence, I advocate a guaranteed annual income which assumes that the antipoverty effort in America is as serious as, for example, the war effort ($80 billion in 1972), the public and private transportation effort (over $120 billion in 1972), and other national priorities. If we really want to solve the problems of the poor, we will free them from dependence on the sweatshops of marginal industries and give them enough income to live a life more consistent with participation in the American economy the rest of us take for granted. Indeed, liberals who give their sanction to guaranteed incomes of less than an adequate level, or who support work incentive programs, unwittingly join hands with conservatives and others in forcing the American poor into a permanent life of penury or occasional employment in demeaning jobs.

I don't think, incidentally, that one can seek refuge in the argument that guaranteeing every family an income of, say, six thousand dollars would be prohibitively costly. One program suggested by James Tobin (see previous footnote), which would guarantee every family thirty-two hundred dollars if no one in the family worked, and would subsidize all families with incomes of less than sixty-four hundred dollars, was estimated to cost an additional seventeen billion dollars more than current programs (in 1968). Thus, a program which raised the thirty-two-hundred-dollar floor to six thousand dollars would cost significantly more, and for the sake of argument, assume such a program would cost fifty billion dollars more than current programs. Can we afford it? It all depends, of course, on where you stand. If you assume that the cause of American poverty lies outside the individual efforts of the poor, the moral imperative to end their problems that derive from low incomes seems overwhelming in an affluent society like our own. And arguing that such a plan is undesirable because it is "inefficient" or "too costly" is only to pay homage to a different morality. My point is only that a liberal antipoverty program which is not aimed clearly and explicitly at the abolition of absolute poverty is simply morally bankrupt and is not defensible in terms of the moral implications of most liberal rhetoric about the "problems of the American poor." And, in my own judgment, liberals who support anything else are engaged unknowingly in a grand subterfuge carried out at the expense of the American poor.

IV. A Final Note on Antipoverty Politics

As I read back over these pages I realize that I have quite forcefully argued against violent revolutionary politics, and that what must have seemed a relentless attack on liberal reform appears to have been only slightly modified in the previous few pages.

In so arguing, I have somewhat cornered myself; at least, I have forced myself to come to terms with a final question: What can I do politically if I want to help abolish poverty and build an egalitarian social order, but have little hope for the long-term success of reform politics and an abhorrence for the idea of barricades in American streets? I will try to answer this question by providing a few examples of political behavior which are nonviolent but which are also inconsistent with the basic assumptions of the liberal reform model. In doing so, I hope to develop a working definition of a third possible political response to American social problems: nonviolent revolutionary politics.

THE ANTIWAR MOVEMENT OF THE 1960's

As an initial example of the nonviolent political style, consider the less militant element in the antiwar protest of the 1960's. This protest, including both its violent and nonviolent factions, was clearly inconsistent with American liberalism, since liberals had, until very recent times, typically been anticommunist and only slightly less pathological than conservatives in their paranoia about world communism. The initial phase of the antiwar protest began with the teach-ins in 1964, of which the first major one was held at the University of Michigan; the teach-ins, plus additional elements of the antiwar protest, quickly spread to other campuses during the next few years. Though, of course, no one knows to what extent the protest movement actually affected policy, everyone now seems to agree that the gradual de-Americanization of the Vietnam war was brought about at least in part by that movement. Moreover, few people doubt that the downfall of Lyndon Johnson was a direct consequence of the essentially nonviolent "Dump Johnson" movement, which was a response to his war politics.

In other words, that element of the antiwar movement which in the 1960's demanded total, immediate withdrawal from Vietnam—a truly revolutionary goal,[7] since it demanded a re-

7. An excellent discussion of the transition in American ideology concerning world communism is Christopher Lasch's "The Revival of Political Controversy in the 1960's." This essay and others by him are compiled in Lasch's *The Agony of the American Left* (New York: Vintage, 1969).

versal of the American political response to revolutionary activity in foreign countries—has certainly failed in terms of its own major aims. Nonetheless, the change that has occurred since the early 1960's in American ideology concerning "world communism" has been profoundly revolutionary (as examples of this change, compare our current attitude about Communist China and Marxist Chile with typical rhetoric about socialist countries just ten years ago). This change in American ideology regarding socialism in other nations is largely the result of the political activity of a relatively small number of mostly nonviolent Americans who refused to accept the conventional wisdom about America's role as the world's toughest and most relentless cop. And even though their political action helped elect their worst enemy as president, the drift in American foreign policy is definitely toward the demands of the antiwar movement in the 1960's.

We Americans with "revolutionary" goals are a crucial element in any long-term evolution of the United States toward a more reasonable social order, for, at last, the politician must compromise with whatever "crazy idea" we can imagine and which we can make part of the platform of a significant number of organized constituents. Like the notion that American anticommunism has been a destructive feature of postwar life, the right of women to vote, the admission of China to the United Nations, the presidential candidacy of a black woman, the legality of labor unions, the income tax, an unbalanced federal budget, and many other accepted facts of American life were at one time the "revolutionary" notion of someone disenchanted with the way the system worked.

Philip Slater, in his book *The Pursuit of Loneliness,* has made the same points concerning the mutual dependence of radicals and liberal reformers, and it is worth quoting him at length. According to Slater:

> The "war on poverty" may have done very little to alleviate poverty and nothing at all to remove its causes, but it raised a lot of expectations, created many visions of the possibilities for change, alerted a large number of people to existing inadequacies in the system and to the relative efficacy of various strategies for

eliminating them. One factor that radicals overlook, in other words, is the educative value of liberal reform, however insignificant that reform may be in terms of institutional change.

Liberal reform and radical change are thus complementary rather than antagonistic. Together they make it possible continually to test the limits of what can be done. Liberals never know whether the door is unlocked because they are afraid to try it. Radicals, on the other hand, miss many opportunities for small advances because they are unwilling to settle for so little. No group can possibly fulfill both these functions—constant testing of the maximum prohibits constant testing of the minimum and vice versa.[8]

THE WOMEN'S LIBERATION MOVEMENT

A second example of nonviolent revolutionary politics is the most recent chapter in the history of the American feminist movement. Most of the rhetoric of the women's movement is based upon the unambiguously revolutionary goal of diminishing the extent to which white American males, operating on the basis of a competitive, aggressive, self-aggrandizing model, dominate our social order. To an important degree, the women's movement seeks to corrode those links we all have to the repressive nuclear family, dominated by males and geared toward maximum production and consumption, an aggressive and chauvinistic approach to other peoples, and the unreflective brutalization of our biosphere. In a very real political sense, therefore, the feminists have joined hands with other revolutionaries in trying to redirect the overall emphasis of our collective social effort.

Moreover, many feminists have concentrated their research efforts on seeking to understand the underlying assumptions of the "masculine mystique" and its relationship to aggressive and violent solutions to personal and social problems. It is not by chance that a population which purchases "Cougars," "Barracudas," and "Mustangs" to drive around in also supports politi-

8. Philip Slater, *The Pursuit of Loneliness* (Boston: Beacon Press, 1970), p. 124.

cians and generals who rejoice in body counts and who consider it a source of great national pride that they have never "lost a war." Feminists, in trying to unravel the connections between, for example, such childish buying habits and such a primitive view of military struggle are providing an invaluable service to all who would understand why we Americans act the way we do and why it is important to change the way we act.

A third example of nonviolent politics which is implicitly (and sometimes explicitly) revolutionary emerged in the 1960's; it is variously identified as the "counterculture," which is made up of "hippies," or "freaks," whose political attitudes comprise what Charles Reich has called, in *The Greening of America,* "Consciousness III." Implicit in such a political style is the assumption that all organized politics are part of a bad ballgame in which only losers win. The counterculture style is probably best exemplified in the public mind by rural communes, urban collectives, long-haired "street people," and "head shops." Few Americans have been able to avoid the relentless bombardment of journalistic accounts of life in the counterculture.

To those of us who are dismayed by the inherent limitations of most organized politics, the appeal of the countercultural political style is quite strong. Indeed, its appeal to me over the past few years has frequently led me to either romanticize its intentions or systematically overestimate its effect on the larger American scene. Nonetheless, I do consider that the young people who have experimented with alternative life styles and who have tried to imagine and experiment with more cooperative working arrangements have been engaged in a truly pioneering adventure. Indeed, my own way of living has been significantly affected by my awareness that younger people, presumably less prepared and less knowledgeable about the world, have actually made the effort to exist outside the American cornucopia.

These comments are not by any means intended to romanticize the counterculture, its communes, its concerts, or its dope-smoking. I am aware that many people who are swept into the counterculture are unable to cope with the larger consequences of its nonstructured life style, and, in many instances, cannot survive a life style unencumbered by straight jobs, school, or other personal responsibilities. Nevertheless, I am, I believe, a freer human being because of the efforts of these young people; I consider this freedom as purchased, to some extent, by the broken spirits of many young people whose fate it has been to show the rest of us what *not* to do when the time comes to drop out of the mainstream of American life. The very existence of alternatives to American middle- and upper-class consumerism has, whether we might have chosen to do so or not, forced us all to reevaluate the basic assumptions of our own life styles. In essence, I am convinced that counterculture activity represents a preeminent example of nonviolent politics, full of possibilities for a revolution in American ideology.

As they said in the nineteen-sixties, in order to change the system, you need to "change people's heads," and to critics of this political stance—liberals who need one's time to stuff envelopes, or others who need one's body for a march on the Pentagon—I can answer only that a necessary preface to the realization of the better American social order about which we all dream is experimentation with life styles alternative to the work-consumption syndrome which basically defines our individual lives. And liberals, *especially,* who combine a public stance of passion for the poor with a personal life style utterly inaccessible to the poor, seem singularly shortsighted and muddleheaded to me. The poor in America, at least most of them, will not in their lifetimes achieve the level of income the rest of us take for granted, nor will the planet supply adequate resources for its population to indulge in the American style of consumerism. *Perhaps, therefore, trying to come to terms with American consumerism, while at the same time working for an adequate guaranteed income, is the best antipoverty strategy in the coming years. It seems very clear to me that income maintenance programs alone do not begin to touch upon a very central aspect of contemporary American social problems.*

Conclusion

The main implication of all this talk about political styles is that there is a considerable variety to choose from and a lot of room for the invention of others. Variety, of course, is necessary, since there are immeasurable differences in the perspectives and personal needs of all those making the choice. What seems most important, as a concluding note, is that the real enemy of the American poor is not the liberal or the nonviolent revolutionary: the real enemy is all those who have *no* commitment to the abolition of poverty, or those who attempt to force others into their own styles, wishing to impose yet another kind of stifling oppression, or revolutionaries who would sacrifice the lives of some in order to make the lives of some others "better." We should recognize this, whether we seek to imagine and make known new and more humane ways in which we can and perhaps must relate to each other, to demonstrate the workability of alternative life styles, to work for liberal political candidates, or to do volunteer work for the local Community Action agency. In doing so, in legitimizing and validating *all* the nonviolent ways in which people engage in antipoverty politics, we can develop workable antipoverty solutions and thus build the basis for a less destructive and more cooperative social order in America.

A SELECTED BIBLIOGRAPHY

The books and articles in this Bibliography have been chosen because they fulfill the following two requirements: *first*, they are concerned with the many dimensions of urban poverty: from its causes to speculations on its cure. Though a disproportionate number of these studies have been written by economists, many are from other disciplines. The study of poverty, if nothing else, demands an interdisciplinary approach, and this list reflects that need. *Second*, each item should be readable to anyone with an interest in the problem. I have intentionally excluded from the list especially abstruse mathematical models and statistical studies, not only because they are incomprehensible to most people but also because they are usually not very useful.

The list should by no means be considered all-inclusive. I have come across these items by glancing through periodicals, from contact with publishers, through casual reading, and in a host of other ways in which one gathers information about any subject. In essence, these are the books and essays which passed through my hands over the past two years or so; some actually changed my mind, and all, to one degree or another, probably had some effect on what has preceded this Bibliography—even those I only scanned briefly to determine the contents. I hope this list proves useful to others concerned with urban poverty.

INTRODUCING THE URBAN PROBLEM

Banfield, Edward. *The Unheavenly City*. Boston:. Little, Brown, 1970.

Baran, Paul, and Paul Sweezy. *Monopoly Capital*. New York Monthly Review Press, 1966.

Canty, Donald. *A Single Society: Alternatives to Urban Apartheid*. New York: Praeger, 1969.

Downs, Anthony. *Urban Problems and Prospects*. Chicago: Markham, 1970.

Eldredge, H. Wentworth, ed. *Taming Megalopolis*. 2 vols. (Vol. 1, *What Is and What Could Be;* Vol. 2, *How to Manage an Urbanized World*.) Garden City: Doubleday, 1967.

Elias, C. E., *et al.*, eds. *Metropolis: Values and Conflicts*. Belmont, Calif.: Wadsworth, 1964.

Gladwin, Thomas. *Poverty U.S.A.* Boston: Little, Brown, 1967.

Gordon, David M., ed. *Problems in Political Economy: An Urban Perspective*. Lexington, Mass.: Heath, 1971.

Grodzins, Morton. *The Metropolitan Area as a Racial Problem*. Pittsburgh: University of Pittsburgh Press, 1958.

Jacobs, Jane. *The Economy of Cities*. New York: Random House, 1969.

———. *The Death and Life of Great American Cities*. New York: Random House, 1961.

Lindsay, John. *The City*. New York: Norton, 1970.

Meyerson, Martin, ed. *The Conscience of the City*. New York: Braziller, 1970.

Netzer, Dick. *Economics and Urban Problems*. New York: Basic Book, 1970.

Piven, Frances Fox, and Richard A. Cloward. *Regulating the Poor: The Functions of Public Welfare*. New York: Random House, 1971.

Sackrey, Charles. "The Urban Problem, Parts 1 and 2," *Valley Review*, February/March, 1971.

Schreiber, Arthur, *et al.*, eds. *Economics of Urban Problems: An Introduction*. Boston: Houghton Mifflin, 1971.

Trachtenberg, Alan, *et al.*, eds. *The City: American Experience*. New York: Oxford University Press, 1971.

Wilson, James Q., ed. *The Metropolitan Enigma*. Garden City: Doubleday, 1970.

Chapter One

COUNTING THE URBAN POOR AND EXPLAINING THEIR POVERTY

A. THE INCOME DIMENSIONS OF URBAN POVERTY

Ackerman, Frank, *et al.* "Income Distribution in the United States," *Review of Radical Political Economics*, Summer, 1971, pp. 20–43.

Downs, Anthony. *Who Are the Urban Poor?* New York: Committee on Economic Development, 1970.

Light, Donald. "Income Distribution: The First Stage in the Consideration of Poverty," *Review of Radical Political Economics*, Summer, 1971, pp. 44–50.

McGuire, Joseph, and Joseph Pichler. *Inequality: The Poor and the Rich in America*. Belmont, Calif.: Wadsworth, 1969.

Ornati, Oscar. "Poverty in the Cities." In *Issues in Urban Economics*, ed. Harvey Perloff and Lowdon Wingo. Baltimore: Johns Hopkins Press, 1968, pp. 335–362.

Orshansky, Mollie. "How Poverty is Measured," *Monthly Labor Review*, February, 1969, pp. 37–41.

Scoville, James G. *Perspectives on Poverty and Income Distribution*. Lexington, Mass.: Heath, 1971.

Thurow, Lester. "The Causes of Poverty," *Quarterly Journal of Economics*, February, 1967, pp. 38–57.

B. THE NON-INCOME DIMENSIONS OF URBAN POVERTY

Anderson, Fred. "Growing Pains of Medical Care, Parts I, II, and III," *New Republic*, January 17, 24, and February 7, 1970.

Anthrop, D. F. "Environmental Noise Pollution: A New Threat to Sanity," *Bulletin of Atomic Scientist*, May, 1969, pp. 11–16.

Block, Richard. "Fear of Crime and Fear of Police," *Social Problems*, Summer, 1971, pp. 91–101.

Bloomberg, Warner, and Henry Schmandt, eds. *Urban Poverty: Its Social and Political Dimensions*. Beverly Hills: Sage Publications, 1970.

Bluestone, Barry. "The Tripartite Economy: Labor Markets and the Working Poor," *Poverty and Human Resources*, July/August, 1970, pp. 15–35.

Bowles, Samuel. "Towards an Educational Production Function." In *Education, Income and Human Capital*, ed. W. Lee Hansen. New York: National Bureau of Economic Research, 1970.

Bregger, John E. "Unemployment Statistics and What They Mean," *Monthly Labor Review*, November, 1971, pp. 22–29.

Caplovitz, David, *The Poor Pay More*. New York: Free Press, 1967.

Center for Policy Study. *The Social Impact of Urban Design*. Chicago: University of Chicago Press, 1971.

Coleman, James, *et al. Equality of Educational Opportunity*. Washington, D.C.: Government Printing Office, 1966.

Coles, Robert. *Migrants, Sharecroppers, Mountaineers*. Vol. 2 of *Children of Crisis*. Boston: Little, Brown, 1972.

———. *The South Goes North*. Vol. 3 of *Children of Crisis*. Boston: Little, Brown, 1972.

Gans, Herbert. "The Uses of Poverty: The Poor Pay All," *Social Policy*, July/August, 1971, pp. 20–24.

Gitlin, Todd, and Nanci Hollander. *Uptown: Poor Whites in Chicago*. New York: Harper & Row, 1970.

Gordon, David. "Class and the Economics of Crime," *Review of Radical Political Economics*, Summer, 1971, pp. 51–75.

Harrington, Michael. *The Other America: Poverty in the United States*. New York: Macmillan, 1962.

Herzog, Elizabeth. "Facts and Fictions about the Poor," *Monthly Labor Review*, February, 1969, pp. 42–49.

Hilaski, Harvey. "How Poverty Area Residents Look for Work," *Monthly Labor Review*, March, 1971, pp. 41–45.

Jones, Peter, ed. *The Robber Barons Revisited*. Lexington, Mass.: Heath, 1968.

Josephson, Matthew. *The Robber Barons*. New York: Harcourt, Brace, 1936.

Kain, John, and John Meyer. "The Interrelationship Between Transportation and Poverty." In *Summary of the Conference on Transportation and Poverty*. Harvard Program on Regional and Urban Economics. Discussion Paper no. 39. Cambridge: Harvard University Press, 1968.

Kain, John F. "The Distribution and Movement of Jobs and Industry." In *The Metropolitan Enigma*, ed. James Q. Wilson. Garden City: Doubleday, 1970.

Kaplan, L. J., and S. Maltise. "The Economics of Loansharking," *American Journal of Economics and Sociology*, July, 1968, pp. 239–252.

Kosa, John, *et al.*, eds. *Poverty and Health: A Sociological Analysis*. Cambridge: Harvard University Press, 1969.

Leacock, Eleanor Burke, ed. *The Culture of Poverty: A Critique*. New York: Simon and Schuster, 1971.

Leavitt, Helen. *Superhighway-Superhoax*. Garden City: Doubleday, 1970.

Lewis, Oscar. *Five Families*. New York: Basic Books, 1959.

———. *La Vida: A Puerto Rican Family in the Culture of Poverty*. New York: Random House, 1966.

Miller, S. M., *et al.* "Creaming the Poor," *Trans-Action*, June, 1970, pp. 38–45.

Moore, William. *The Vertical Ghetto: Everyday Life in an Urban Project*. New York: Random House, 1968.

Moynihan, Daniel P., ed. *On Understanding Poverty: Perspectives from the Social Sciences*. New York: Basic Books, 1969.

Ornati, Oscar, *et al. Transportation Needs of the Poor: A Case Study of New York City.* New York: Praeger, 1970.

Reichley, James. "The Texas Banker Who Bought Politicians," *Fortune,* December, 1971, pp. 94–99, 143–146.

Schrag, Peter. "Why Our Schools Have Failed," *Commentary,* March, 1968, pp. 31–38.

Seligman, Ben B. *Aspects of Poverty: Selected Studies in Social Problems.* New York: Crowell, 1968.

Smith, Richard. "The Incredible Electrical Conspiracy, Parts I and II," *Fortune,* April and May, 1961.

Southworth, Gayle. "Some Notes on the Political Economy of Pollution," *Review of Radical Political Economics,* Summer, 1970, pp. 74–87.

Stanley, W. O., *et al. Social Foundations of Education.* New York: Dryden, 1956.

Sutherland, Edwin. *White Collar Crime.* New York: Dryden, 1949.

Sternlieb, George. *The Tenement Landlord.* New Brunswick: Rutgers University Press, 1969.

Strauss, Anselm L., ed. *Where Medicine Fails.* Chicago: Aldine, 1970.

Suttles, Gerald. *The Social Order of the Slum.* Chicago: University of Chicago Press, 1970.

Tiffany, Donald, *et al. The Unemployed: A Social-Psychological Portrait.* Englewood Cliffs: Prentice-Hall, 1970.

Tunley, Roul. *The American Health Scandal.* New York: Harper & Row, 1966.

Weaver, Thomas, and Alvin Magid, eds. *Poverty: New Interdisciplinary Perspectives.* San Francisco: Chandler, 1969.

Chapter Two

THE POVERTY OF URBAN BLACK PEOPLE

Beal, Frances M. "Double Jeopardy: To Be Black and Female." In *Sisterhood Is Powerful,* ed. Robin Morgan. New York: Random House, 1971.

Becker, Gary S. *The Economics of Discrimination.* 2nd ed. Chicago: University of Chicago Press, 1971.

Browne, Robert. "Barriers to Black Participation in the United States Economy," *Review of Black Political Economy,* Autumn, 1970, pp. 57–67.

Cohen, Benjamin I. "Another Theory of Residential Segregation," *Land Economics,* August, 1971, pp. 314–315.

Day, R. H. "The Economics of Technological Change and the Demise of the Sharecropper," *American Economic Review*, June, 1967, pp. 427–449.

Demarest, David, and Lois Lamdin, eds. *The Ghetto Reader*. New York: Random House, 1970.

Fusfeld, Daniel. *The Basic Economics of the Urban and Racial Crisis*. Conference Papers of the Union of Radical Political Economists, Reprint no. 1. Ann Arbor, 1968.

Goldman, Peter. *Report from Black America*. New York: Simon and Schuster, 1971.

Grimshaw, Allen, ed. *Racial Violence in the United States*. Chicago: Aldine, 1969.

——. "Discrimination and Income Differentials," *American Economic Review*, June, 1970, pp. 396–408.

Heller, Walter W. "Economics of the Race Problem," *Social Research*, Winter, 1970, pp. 495–510.

Jacobs, Paul. *Prelude To Riot: A View of Urban America from the Bottom*. New York: Random House, 1968.

Kain, John F. *Race and Poverty: The Economics of Discrimination*. Englewood Cliffs: Prentice-Hall, 1969.

——. *Theories of Residential Location and Realities of Race*. Harvard Program on Regional and Urban Economics, Discussion Paper no. 47. Cambridge: Harvard University Press, 1969.

——. "Housing Segregation, Negro Employment and Metropolitan Decentralization," *Quarterly Journal of Economics*, May, 1968, pp. 175–197.

Kain, John F., and J. Quigley. *Housing Market Discrimination, Homeownership and Savings Behavior*. Harvard Program on Regional and Urban Economics, Discussion Paper no. 58. Cambridge: Harvard University Press, 1970.

Labrie, Peter. "Black Central Cities: Dispersal or Rebuilding, Parts I and II," *Review of Black Political Economy*, Autumn, 1970, pp. 3–27, Winter/Spring, 1971, pp. 78–99.

Liebow, Elliot. *Tally's Corner: A Study of Negro Streetcorner Men*. Boston: Little, Brown, 1967.

Marshall, Ray, and Lamond Godwin. *Cooperatives and Rural Poverty in the South*. Baltimore: Johns Hopkins University Press, 1971.

Michelson, Stephan. "On Income Differentials by Race: An Analysis and a Suggestion," *Review of Radical Political Economics*, December, 1968, pp. 85–121.

Osofsky, Gilbert. *Harlem: The Making of a Ghetto*. New York: Harper & Row, 1966.

Rainwater, Lee, and William Yancey. *The Moynihan Report and the Politics of Controversy*. Cambridge: MIT Press, 1967.

Rainwater, Lee. *Behind Ghetto Walls: Black Family Life in a Federal Slum*. New York: Aldine, 1970.

Report of the National Advisory Commission on Civil Disorders. New York: Bantam, 1968.

Ross, Arthur, and Herbert Hill, eds. *Employment, Race and Poverty*. New York: Harcourt, Brace & World, 1967.

Sackrey, Charles. "Economics and Black Poverty," *Review of Black Political Economy*, Winter/Spring, 1971, pp. 47–64.

Schiller, Bradley. "Class Discrimination versus Racial Discrimination," *Review of Economic Studies*, August, 1971, pp. 263–269.

Sherman, Richard, ed. *The Negro and the City*. Englewood Cliffs: Prentice-Hall, 1970.

Silberman, Charles. *Crisis in Black and White*. New York: Random House, 1964.

Tabb, William K. *The Political Economy of the Black Ghetto*. New York: Norton, 1970.

———. "Race Relations Models and Social Change," *Social Problems*, Spring, 1971, pp. 431–443.

Taueber, Karl and Alma. *Negroes in Cities: Residential Segregation and Neighborhood Change*. Chicago: Aldine, 1965.

Thurow, Lester. *Poverty and Discrimination*. Washington, D.C.: Brookings Institution, 1969.

Vowels, Robert. "The Political Economy of American Racism: Non-black Decision-Making and Black Economic Status," *Review of Black Political Economy*, Summer, 1971, pp. 3–39.

Chapter Three

ECONOMICS AND BLACK POVERTY: THE METHODOLOGY
OF CONTEMPORARY LIBERAL ECONOMICS

Brennan, Michael. *A Preface to Econometrics*. 2nd ed. Cincinnati: South-Western, 1965.

Broffenbrenner, Martin. "Radical Economics in America: A 1970 Survey," *Journal of Economic Literature*, September, 1970, pp. 747–766.

Gottlieb, Manuel. "Mukerjee: Economics Become Social Science," *Journal of Economic Issues*, December, 1971, pp. 33–53.

Gurley, John. "The State of Political Economics," *American Economic Review*, May, 1971, pp. 53–62.

Heilbroner, Robert, and Arthur Ford. *Is Economics Relevant?* Pacific Palisades, Calif.: Goodyear, 1971.

Hinckley, Robert. "Some Comments on Economic Methodology." (Copy available on request from Charles Sackrey, Smith College, Northampton, Massachusetts.)

Lansing, John, and James Morgan. *Economic Survey Methods.* Ann Arbor: University of Michigan, Institute for Social Research, 1971.

Linbeck, Assar. *The Political Economy of the New Left: An Outsider's View.* New York: Harper & Row, 1971.

Lowe, Adolph. *On Economic Knowledge: Toward a Science of Political Economics.* New York: Harper & Row, 1965.

Maslow, Abraham. *The Psychology of Science.* New York: Harper & Row, 1966.

Morgenstern, Oskar. *On the Accuracy of Economic Observation.* 2nd ed. Princeton: Princeton University Press, 1963.

"On Radical Paradigms in Economics," *Review of Radical Political Economics,* July, 1971, a special issue on methodology.

Roszak, Theodore. *The Making of a Counterculture.* Garden City: Doubleday, 1969.

Schnore, Leo, ed. *Social Science and the City.* New York: Praeger, 1968.

Stretton, Hugh. *The Political Sciences.* New York: Basic Books, 1969.

Sweezy, Paul. *The Theory of Capitalist Development.* New York: Oxford University Press, 1942.

Chapter Four

LIBERAL SOLUTIONS FOR URBAN POVERTY

A. THE LIBERAL PERSPECTIVE AND ITS CRITICS

Dahl, Robert. *A Preface to Democratic Theory.* Chicago: University of Chicago Press, 1956.

——. *Pluralist Democracy in the United States.* Chicago: Rand McNally, 1967.

Domhoff, William G. *The Higher Circles.* New York: Random House, 1971.

——. *Who Rules America?* Englewood Cliffs: Prentice-Hall, 1967.

Donovan, John C. *The Politics of Poverty.* New York: Western, 1967.

Friedman, Milton. *Capitalism and Freedom.* Chicago: University of Chicago Press, 1962.

Galbraith, John K. *The Concept of Countervailing Power*. Boston: Houghton Mifflin, 1952.

Liebhafsky, H. H. *American Government and Business*. New York: Wiley, 1971.

Lundberg, Ferdinand. *The Rich and the Super-Rich*. New York: Bantam, 1968.

Mills, C. Wright. *The Power Elite*. New York: Oxford University Press, 1956.

Rose, Arnold. *The Power Structure*. New York: Oxford University Press, 1967.

Samuelson, Paul. *Economics*. 6th ed. New York: McGraw-Hill, 1967.

Schrag, Peter. "Common Cause: New Paths for WASP Elites," *Social Policy*, November/December, 1971, pp. 29–35.

B. LABOR MARKET POLICIES

Appel, G. L., and R. E. Schlendar. "Michigan's Experience with Work Incentives," *Monthly Labor Review*, September, 1971, pp. 15–22.

Berg, Ivar. *Education and Jobs: The Great Training Robbery*. New York: Praeger, 1970.

Chalmers, James, and Fred Leonard. *Economic Principles: Macroeconomic Theory and Policy*. New York: Macmillan, 1971.

Dale, Edwin, Jr. "The Great Unemployment Fallacy," *New Republic*, September 5, 1964, pp. 10–12.

Ginzberg, Eli. "The Outlook for Educated Manpower," *The Public Interest*, Winter, 1972, pp. 100–111.

Hale, Carl. "Impact of Federal Policy and Technological Change on Regional and Urban Training Programs," *Land Economics*, February, 1971, pp. 24–35.

Harrison, Bennett. "National Manpower and Public Service Employment," *New Generation*, Winter, 1971, pp. 3–14.

Hickey, Joseph. "A Report on State Unemployment Insurance Laws," *Monthly Labor Review*, January, 1972, pp. 40–50.

Kain, John F. "Coping with Ghetto Employment," *Journal of the American Institute of Planners*, March, 1969, pp. 80–83.

Killingsworth, Charles C. "Jobs and Income for Negroes," Joint Publication of the Institute of Labor and Industrial Relations, University of Michigan, Wayne State University, and the National Manpower Policy Task Force, Papers in Human Resources and Industrial Relations, no. 6. Washington, D.C., 1968.

Kitgaard, Robert. "The Dual Labor Market and Manpower Policy," *Monthly Labor Review*, November, 1971, pp. 45–48.

Marien, Michael. "Beyond Credentialism: The Future of Social Selection," *Social Policy,* September and October, 1971, pp. 14–21.

McVay, Roberta. "Job Training Programs in Urban Poverty Areas," *Monthly Labor Review,* August, 1971, pp. 36–41.

Nadler, Leonard. "Helping the Hard-Core Adjust to the World of Work," *Harvard Business Review,* March/April, 1970, pp. 117–126.

Research and Policy Committee. *Training and Jobs for the Urban Poor.* New York: Committee on Economic Development, 1970.

Rosen, Sumner M. "Manpower Issues for the City," *Urban Affairs,* September, 1970, pp. 22–32.

Wellman, David. *Putting on the Poverty Program.* Ann Arbor: Radical Education Project, n.d. [1968].

C. INCOME MAINTENANCE PROGRAMS

Becker, Joseph. *Guaranteed Annual Income for the Unemployed.* Baltimore: Johns Hopkins Press, 1968.

Coser, Lewis. "What Do the Poor Need?" *Dissent,* October, 1971, pp. 485–491.

Glassman, Carol. "Women and the Welfare System." In *Sisterhood is Powerful,* ed. Robin Morgan. New York: Random House, 1970.

Hildebrand, George. *Poverty, Income Maintenance and the Negative Income Tax.* Ithaca: Cornell University Press, 1967.

"Income Maintenance Programs," *American Economic Review* (papers and proceedings, panel discussion, May, 1971), pp. 15–42.

Levitan, Sar. *Programs in Aid of the Poor for the 1970's.* Baltimore: Johns Hopkins Press, 1969.

Research and Policy Committee. *Improving the Public Welfare System.* New York: Committee on Economic Development, 1970.

Segal, Judith. *Food for the Hungry: The Reluctant Society.* Baltimore: Johns Hopkins Press, 1970.

Spilerman, Seymour, and David Elesh. "Alternative Conceptions of Poverty and Their Implications for Income Maintenance," *Social Problems,* Winter, 1971, pp. 358–372.

Steiner, Gilbert. *The State of Welfare.* Washington, D.C.: Brookings Institution, 1971.

Wiley, George, and Jonathan Kaufman. "Adequate Income versus Nixon's Welfare Reform," *Social Policy,* November/December, 1970, pp. 33–35.

D. HOUSING POLICIES

Abrams, Charles. *Homeownership for the Poor: A Program for Philadelphia*. New York: Praeger, 1970.

deLeeuw, Frank, and Nkanta F. Ekanem. "The Supply of Rental Housing," *American Economic Review*, December, 1971, pp. 806–817.

Freedman, Leonard. *Public Housing: The Politics of Poverty*. New York: Holt, Rinehart and Winston, 1969.

Fried, Joseph. *Housing Crisis, U.S.A.* New York: Praeger, 1971.

Friedan, Bernard, and Jo Ann Newman. "Homeownership for the Poor?" *Trans-Action*, October, 1970, pp. 47–53.

Hartman, Chester W., and Gregg Carr. "Housing the Poor," *Trans-Action*, December, 1969, pp. 49–53.

Hunter, Oakley. "Boosting Housing for the Inner City," *Nation's Cities*, December, 1971, pp. 11–12, 23.

Lansing, John, *et al. New Homes for Poor People: A Study in Chains of Moves*. Ann Arbor: University of Michigan, Survey Research Center, 1969.

Lebergott, Stanley. "Slum Housing: A Proposal," *Journal of Political Economy*, November/December, 1970, pp. 1362–1366.

National Commission on Urban Problems. *Building the American City*. New York: Praeger, 1969.

Schucsheim, Morton J. "Why We Have Not Built More Houses," *The Public Interest*, Spring, 1970, pp. 18–30.

Starr, Roger. "Which of the Poor Shall Live in Public Housing?" *The Public Interest*, Spring, 1971, pp. 116–124.

Stegman, Michael. "The New Mythology of Housing," *Trans-Action*, January, 1970, pp. 55–62.

Subcommittee on Urban Affairs, Joint Economic Committee, 91st Congress. *Industrialized Housing*, Parts I and II. Washington, D.C.: Government Printing Office, 1969.

Sullivan, Donald. *Cooperative Housing and Community Development: A Comparative Evaluation of Three Housing Projects in East Harlem*. New York: Praeger, 1971.

Taggart, Robert, III. *Low Income Housing: A Critique of Federal Aid*. Baltimore: Johns Hopkins Press, 1970.

Welfeld, Irving. "Toward a New Federal Housing Policy," *The Public Interest*, Spring, 1970, pp. 31–43.

Wendt, Paul. "The Determination of National Housing Policy," *Land Economics*, August, 1969, pp. 323–332.

E. URBAN RENEWAL AND SLUM REDEVELOPMENT

Anderson, Martin. *The Federal Bulldozer.* Cambridge: MIT Press, 1964.

Bellush, Jewel, and Murray Hausknecht, eds. *Urban Renewal: People, Politics, and Planning.* Garden City: Doubleday, 1967.

Berger, Curtis, *et al.* "Slum Area Rehabilitation by Private Enterprise," *Columbia Law Review,* May, 1969, pp. 739–769.

Berry, Brian, *et al. The Impact of Urban Renewal on Small Business.* Chicago: University of Chicago Press, 1968.

Childs, Gerald. "Efficient Reallocation of Land in Urban Renewal," *Western Economics Journal,* September, 1969, pp. 211–222.

Clark, Kenneth, and Jeannette Hopkins. *A Relevant War Against Poverty.* New York: Harper & Row, 1968.

Clinard, Marshall B. *Slums and Community Development.* New York: Free Press, 1966.

Edel, Matthew. "Urban Renewal and Land Use Conflicts," *Review of Radical Political Economics,* Summer, 1971, pp. 76–89.

Eichler, Edward P., and Marshall Kaplan. *The Community Builders.* Berkeley: University of California Press, 1967.

Friedman, Lawrence M. *Government and Slum Housing.* Chicago: Rand-McNally, 1968.

Huxtable, Ada Louise. *Will They Ever Finish Bruckner Boulevard?* New York: Macmillan, 1970.

Kaplan, Harold. *Urban Renewal Politics: Slum Clearance in Newark.* New York: Columbia University Press, 1963.

Kaplan, Samuel. "Bridging the Gap from Rhetoric: New York State Urban Development Corporation," *The Architectural Forum,* November, 1969, pp. 70–73.

Lowi, Theodore. "Apartheid, U.S.A.," *Trans-Action,* February, 1970, pp. 32–39.

Moynihan, Daniel P. *Maximum Feasible Misunderstanding.* New York: Free Press, 1969.

President's Task Force on Model Cities. *Model Cities: A Step Towards the New Federalism.* Washington, D.C.: Government Printing Office, 1970.

Rothenberg, Jerome. "Urban Renewal Programs." In *Measuring Benefits of Government Investments,* ed. Robert Dorfman. Washington, D.C.: Brookings Institution, 1965, pp. 292–367.

Schickel, Richard. "New York's Mr. Urban Renewal," *New York Times Magazine,* March 1, 1970, pp. 30–42.

Wilson, James Q., ed. *Urban Renewal: The Record and the Contro-versy.* Cambridge: MIT Press, 1967.

Yandle, Bruce. "Urban Renewal: The Precondition for Take Off," *Land Economics*, November, 1970, pp. 484–486.

F. ECONOMIC AND POLITICAL DEVELOPMENT
OF BLACK NEIGHBORHOODS

Anderson, Talmadge. "Black Economic Liberation under Capitalism," *Black Scholar*, October, 1970, pp. 11–16.

Andreasen, Allen. *Inner City Business: A Case Study of Buffalo, New York.* New York: Praeger, 1971.

Bell, Carolyn Shaw. *The Economics of the Ghetto.* New York: Western, 1970.

Bell, Inge Powell. *CORE and the Strategy of Nonviolence.* New York: Random House, 1968.

Berman, Jeffrey A. "The Birth of a Black Business," *Harvard Business Review*, September/October, 1970, pp. 4–8, 12–19, 152.

Blaustein, Arthur I. "What is Community Economic Development?" *Urban Affairs*, September, 1970, pp. 52–70.

Brann, W. Paul, *et al. Community Economic Development Efforts: Five Case Studies*, Committee for Economic Development, Report no. 18s. New York, 1964.

Brower, Michael, and Doyle Little. "White Help for Black Business," *Harvard Business Review*, May/June, 1970, pp. 4–16, 163–164.

Cross, Theodore. *Black Capitalism: Strategy for Business in the Ghetto.* New York: Atheneum, 1969.

Davidoff, Linda and Paul, and Neil Gold. "The Suburbs Have to Open Their Gates," *New York Times Magazine*, November 7, 1971, pp. 40–60.

Davis, Frank G. "Problems of Economic Growth in the Black Community: Some Alternative Hypotheses," *Review of Black Political Economy*, Summer, 1971, pp. 75–107.

Foley, Eugene. "The Negro Businessman," *Daedalus*, Winter, 1966, pp. 107–144.

———. *The Achieving Ghetto.* Washington, D.C.: National, 1968.

Frazier, E. Franklin. *Black Bourgeoisie.* New York: Free Press, 1957.

Haddad, William, and Douglas Pugh, eds. *Black Economic Development.* Englewood Cliffs: Prentice-Hall, 1969.

Henderson, William, and Larry Ledebur. *Economic Disparity: Problems and Strategies for Black America.* New York: Free Press, 1970.

Kain, John F., and Joseph J. Persky. "Alternatives to the Gilded Ghetto," *The Public Interest,* Winter, 1969, pp. 74–87.

Killens, John O. "Black Labor and the Black Liberation Movement," *Black Scholar,* October, 1970, pp. 33–39.

Levitan, Sar. "Community Self-Determination and Entrepreneurship: Their Promise and Limitations," *Poverty and Human Resources,* January/February, 1969, pp. 16–24.

———, et al. *Economic Opportunity in the Ghetto: The Partnership of Government and Business.* Baltimore: Johns Hopkins Press, 1970.

Marshall, Ray. *The Negro Worker.* New York: Random House, 1967.

Mitchell, Daniel. "Black Economic Development and Income Drain: The Case of the Numbers," *Review of Black Political Economy,* Autumn, 1970, pp. 47–56.

Pascal, Anthony. "Black Gold and Black Capitalism," *The Public Interest,* Spring, 1970, pp. 111–123.

Pinkney, Alphonso, and Roger Woock. *Poverty and Politics in Harlem: Report on Project Uplift, 1965.* New Haven: Yale University Press, 1970.

Reiss, Albert J., and Howard Aldrich. "Absentee Ownership and Management in Black Ghetto: Social and Economic Consequences," *Social Problems,* Winter, 1971, pp. 319–339.

Spratlen, Thaddeus. "Ghetto Economic Development: Content and Character of the Literature," *Review of Black Political Economy,* Summer, 1971, pp. 43–71.

Sturdivant, Frederick, ed. *The Ghetto Marketplace.* New York: Free Press, 1969.

Tabb, William. "Government Incentives to Private Industry to Locate in Urban Poverty Areas," *Land Economics,* November, 1969, pp. 392–399.

———. *The Political Economy of the Black Ghetto.* New York: Norton, 1970.

Timmons, Jeffrey. "Black Is Beautiful: Is It Bountiful?" *Harvard Business Review,* November/December, 1971, pp. 81–92.

Toll, Seymour. *Zoned America.* New York: Grossman, 1969.

Vatter, Harold J., and Thomas Palm. *The Economics of Black America.* New York: Harcourt Brace Jovanovich, 1972.

Vietorisz, Thomas, and Benjamin Harrison. *A Proposed Investment Program for the Economic Development of Central Harlem.* New York: Praeger, 1970.

Winegarden, C. R. "Industrialization of the Black Economy: Industry Selection," *Review of Black Political Economy,* Autumn, 1970, pp. 28–46.

Zedler, Raymond. "Residential Desegregation: Can Nothing Be Accomplished?" *Urban Affairs*, March, 1970, pp. 265–277.

Zeul, Carolyn, and Craig Humphrey. "The Integration of Blacks in Suburban Neighborhoods," *Social Problems*, Spring, 1971, pp. 462–474.

G. OTHER USEFUL ITEMS

"Achieving Revenue Sharing," *Current*, April, 1971, pp. 40–52.

Banfield, Edward. "Revenue Sharing in Theory and Practice," *The Public Interest*, Spring, 1971, pp. 33–45.

Crecine, J. P. *Financing the Metropolis: Public Policy in Urban Economics*. Beverly Hills: Sage, 1970.

Gottlieb, David. "VISTA: Pepsi and Poverty," *Trans-Action*, February, 1972, pp. 6–8.

Kershaw, Joseph. *Government Against Poverty*. Chicago: Markham, 1970.

Levitan, Sar. *The Great Society's Poor Law: A New Approach to Poverty*. Baltimore: Johns Hopkins Press, 1969.

Marmor, Theodore, ed. *Poverty Policy*. Chicago: Aldine, 1971.

Maxwell, James A. *Financing State and Local Governments*. Rev. ed. Washington, D.C.: Brookings Institution, 1969.

Oates, Wallace. *Fiscal Federalism*. New York: Harcourt Brace Jovanovich, 1971.

Perloff, Harvey S., and Richard P. Nathan. *Revenue Sharing and the City*. Baltimore: Johns Hopkins Press, 1968.

Seligman, Ben B., ed. *Poverty as a Public Issue*. New York: Free Press, 1965.

Smith, Francis X. "New York City's Fiscal Situation," *American Journal of Economics and Sociology*, January, 1970, pp. 49–54.

Steiner, Gilbert. *The State of Welfare*. Washington, D.C.: Brookings Institution, 1971.

Chapter Five

BEYOND LIBERAL REFORM: REVOLUTION AND OTHER SUGGESTIONS

Allen, Robert L. *Black Awakening in Capitalist America*. Garden City: Doubleday, 1970.

Anderson, Jervis. "The Agonies of Black Militancy," *Dissent*, February, 1971, pp. 23–29.

Bachrach, Peter, and Morton Baratz. *Power and Poverty: Theory and Practice*. New York: Oxford University Press, 1970.

Blauner, Robert. "Internal Colonialism and Ghetto Revolt," *Social Problems*, Spring, 1969, pp. 393–408.

Boggs, James. *Racism and the Class Struggle: Further Notes from a Black Worker's Notebook*. New York: Monthly Review Press, 1970.

Calvert, Greg, and Carol Neiman. *A Disrupted History: The New Left and the New Capitalism*. New York: Random House, 1971.

Epstein, Edward Jay. "A Reporter at Large: "The Panthers and the Police: A Pattern of Genocide?" *New Yorker*, February 13, 1971, pp. 45–77.

Franklin, Raymond. "The Political Economy of Black Power," *Social Problems*, Winter, 1969, pp. 286–301.

Goodman, Paul and Percival. *Communitas*. New York: Random House, 1947.

Guerin, Daniel. *Anarchism: From Theory to Practice*. New York: Monthly Review Press, 1970.

Hamilton, David. "The Paper War on Poverty," *Journal of Economic Issues*, September, 1971, pp. 72–79.

Horowitz, Irving. "Separate But Equal: Revolution and Counterrevolution in the American City," *Social Problems*, Winter, 1970, pp. 294–313.

Jackson, George. "The Last Words of a Soledad Brother," *Esquire*, March, 1972, pp. 110–111, 159.

Kahn, Si. *How People Get Power: Organizing Oppressed Communities for Action*. New York: McGraw-Hill, 1970.

Keddie, Wells. "Socialist Academics and the Labor Movement," *Monthly Review*, February, 1972, pp. 44–53.

Larner, Jeremy, and Irving Howe, eds. *Poverty: Views from the Left*. New York: Apollo, 1968.

Lasch, Christopher. *The Agony of the American Left*. New York: Vintage, 1969.

Mandel, Ernest. *Marxist Economic Theory*. New York: Monthly Review Press, 1969.

Merkx, Gilbert. "Revolution in America," *Monthly Review*, January, 1972, pp. 28–43.

Miliband, Ralph. *The State in Capitalist Society*. New York: Basic Books, 1969.

Mumford, Lewis. *The Urban Prospect*. New York: Harcourt, Brace and World, 1968.

Nachman, Larry. "Strategies for Radical Social Change," *Social Policy*, September/October, 1971, pp. 52–57.

Ofari, Earl. *The Myth of Black Capitalism*. New York: Monthly Review Press, 1970.

Roosevelt, Frank. "Market Socialism: A Humane Economy?" *Journal of Economic Issues*, December, 1969, pp. 3–20.

Silverman, Sondra, ed. *The Black Revolt and Democratic Politics*. Lexington, Mass.: Heath, 1970.

Skinner, B. F. *Walden Two*. New York: Macmillan, 1960.

Slater, Philip. *The Pursuit of Loneliness*. Boston: Beacon Press, 1970.

Solnit, Albert. "Wear and Tear in the Communes," *Nation*, April 26, 1971, pp. 524–527.

"Strategies for Radical Social Change: A Symposium," *Social Policy*, November/December, 1970, pp. 9–23.

Theobold, Robert. *Alternative Future for America*. Chicago: Swallow, 1970.

Wachtel, Howard. "Looking at Poverty from a Radical Perspective," *Review of Radical Political Economics*, Summer, 1971, pp. 1–19.

Wiebenon, John. "Planning and Using Resurrection City," *Journal of the American Institute of Planners*, November, 1969, pp. 405–412.

Wilczynski, J. *The Economics of Socialism*. Chicago: Aldine, 1970.

Wilson, Charles E. "Black Nationalism at the Crossroads," *Social Policy*, September/October, 1970, pp. 45–47.

Wright, Frank Lloyd. *The Living City*. New York: Horizon, 1958.

INDEX